Arctic 2 Antarctic

A *Celtic Spirit of Fastnet* Adventure

Celtic Spirit
OF FASTNET

PUBLISHED IN 2008 BY
The Collins Press
West Link Park
Doughcloyne
Wilton
Cork

British Library Cataloguing in Publication Data

Holland, Michael
Arctic2Antarctic : a Celtic Spirit of Fastnet voyage
1. Celtic Spirit of Fastnet (Yacht) 2. Sailing 3. Ocean travel
I. Title II. King, Janet
910.4'5

ISBN-13: 9781905172641

Design concept and layout: Janet King
Printed in Italy by Printer Trento

www.arctic2antarctic.com

Contents

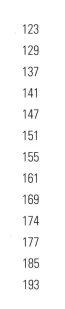

Left: *Crew silhoutte.*
Above: *Lemaire Channel, Antarctica.*

This book is dedicated to all the crew of Celtic Spirit.

A special thanks

The crew would like to thank Michael Holland, owner and skipper of *Celtic Spirit of Fastnet* for his vision to undertake this trip. Not only did he reorganise his business commitments but took time out of his personal life in order to lead us all in this adventure. We thank his wife Carol, children Michael and Sofie, and family for putting up with his time away. Michael is a man of incredible drive and determination. He is a problem solver and lateral thinker and capable of handling any situation that presents itself rationally and calmly. We thank him for his ability to lead in a firm but fair manner, for allowing us this opportunity to join him on board, for his commitment to providing the boat and putting her through refit in order to have her completely seaworthy and looking after us and feeding us whilst on board. He has provided us with laughter and fun wherever we have gone. He chose a crew who were able to get on well together and willingly tackle any task needed. Each person brings a different point of view and skill to the boat. Without Michael this journey would not have happened and for most crew it has significantly changed our lives. We will remember him and *Celtic Spirit* forever and hope that this book will reflect our memories in years to come.

The people who made up the crew and immersed themselves in life on board and enjoyed the journey wholeheartedly need a special mention. Without them Michael could not have made this trip. There were those crew involved in the detail of organisation in preparing the boat. Ansis, who spent months in Lymington overseeing the refit alongside surveyors John and Joanna Freeman who, throughout the voyage, were on call to deal with technical issues. We thank the crew who joined us en route and adapted quickly to life onboard. It is not always easy to place yourself in a confined space with people you do not know and get on with dealing with watches and cooking as well as sailing the boat.

We thank all the people that we met along our journey. From the people in Isafjordur and Reykjavik in Iceland to the Rias of north west Spain, the beaches of Cape Verdes, the pontoon in Salvador, the restaurant in Buzios, the friends we made in Rio de Janeiro, Antarctica, Ushuaia and South Georgia. We thank all the people involved in the production of this book and those who have made it possible. Once again thank you Michael Holland.

Janet King *(on behalf of the crew and skipper)*

It was wonderful to play a part in this journey, my only regret is that I was not there for every mile logged and every watch kept. My most sincere thanks to the skipper and crew of the Celtic Spirit for a voyage I will always remember and that has shaped my life in the most unexpected and wonderful of ways.

Jon Wright

Introduction

The adventure

This Arctic to Antarctic adventure was inspired by a fascinating voyage from Dingle, Ireland, to north west Greenland in the summer of 2003. Sailing among icebergs and the truly spectacular scenery of that remote and sparsely populated country set the scene for a longing to do even more adventurous sailing. Dense fog, ice and the possibility of colliding with bergy bits that could lead to dire consequences did not deter us. This was a challenge worth crossing oceans for.

In July 2005 *Celtic Spirit of Fastnet* left Ireland to sail for Iceland and in so doing crossed the Arctic Circle. She returned to Ireland before undergoing a major refit in Lymington, England in preparation for her voyage to the Antarctic. *Celtic Spirit* then sailed south to Antarctica, visiting the north west of Spain, Portugal, the Canary Islands, the Cape Verde Islands, Salvador and Rio de Janeiro in Brazil, and Mar del Plata and Ushuaia in Argentina before sailing onwards to Antarctica. She sailed back to Ushuaia to provision and then moved on to Puerto Williams in Chile. From Puerto Williams it was out into the Southern Ocean and on to South Georgia. It had been planned to sail to Cape Town, South Africa but plans changed and instead the boat returned to Argentina, sailing into Beunos Aires. From there *Celtic Spirit* returned to Uruguay and sailed up the coast, stopping at various destinations, before finally dropping anchor in the Caribbean. She covered more than 19,000 miles on her voyage of nearly two years.

Opposite page: *The islands around Parati, Brazil as seen from the bow of* Celtic Spirit.

The route

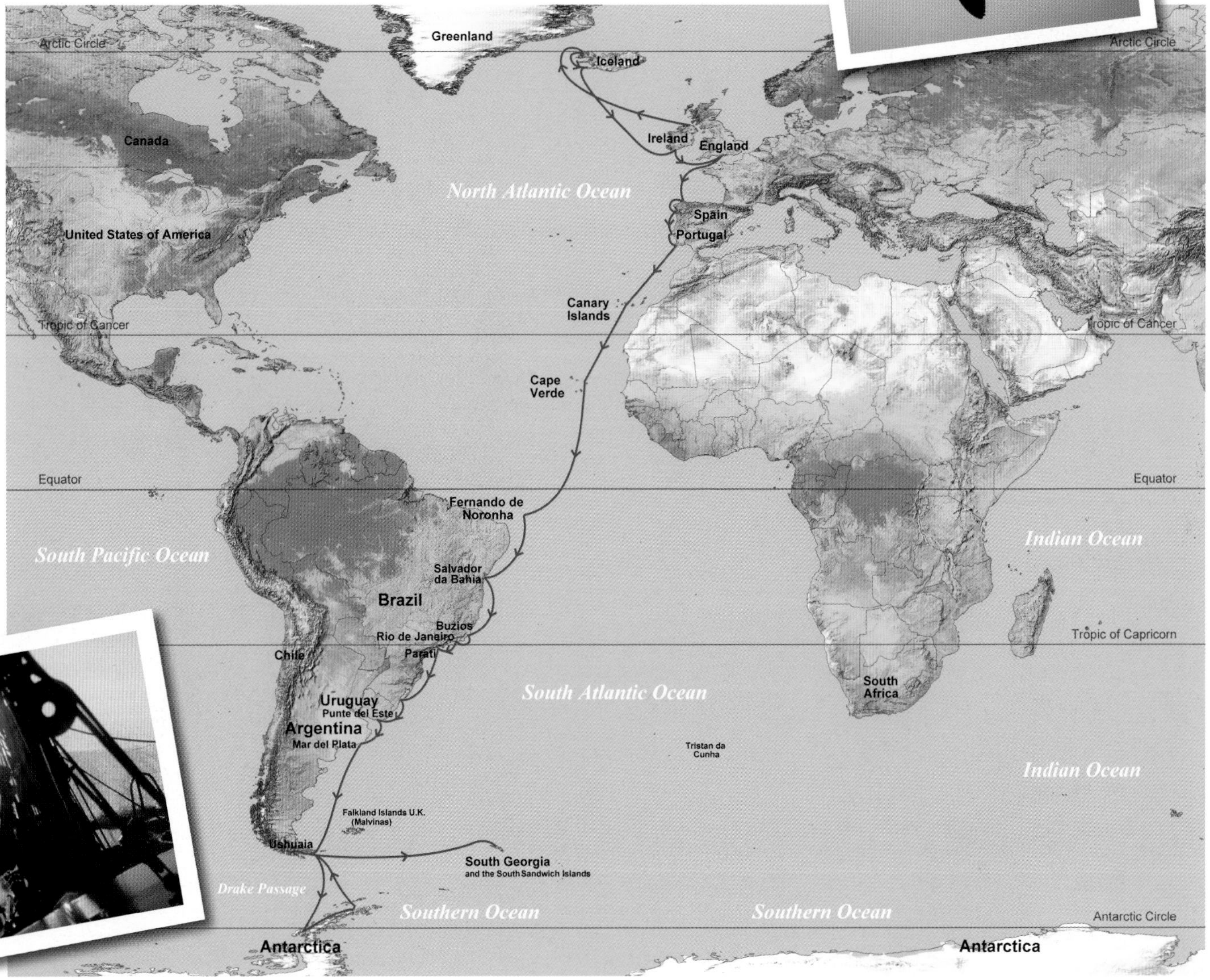

CELTIC SPIRIT

The boat

Celtic Spirit of Fastnet is a 71-foot aluminium ketch, designed by Ed Dubois and built by Pendennis shipyard in Falmouth, Cornwall in the United Kingdom. She was originally owned by a Chilean who had her built for sailing in the Southern Ocean, and was aptly named *Beagle*. Down below she features a split-level main section with dining area and a saloon raised from the crew mess and galley. The boat can sleep nine persons in five cabins. The galley is extremely well equipped with gas hob and large fridge and freezer. *Celtic Spirit* is ketch rigged and carries a large wardrobe of sails. The transom has a large hydraulically operated platform which acts as a dinghy dock for the tender and also allows for easy access to swimming, diving and fishing. *Celtic Spirit* was specially refitted for sailing in extreme latitudes between September 2005 and May 2006.

Length: 21.6 m / 71 feet
Beam: 5.5 m / 18 feet
Draft: 2.8 m / 9 feet 2 inches
Fuel: 4,000 litres
Water: 4,000 litres
Displacement: 46 tons
Boat systems: Iridium Satellite phone, SSB and VHF radios; Transas Navigation System; Furuno Radar with ARPA; Twin 135 hp Perkins Engines; Twin Generators; Spectra Watermaker.

Opposite page: Celtic Spirit *at anchor in Brazil.*

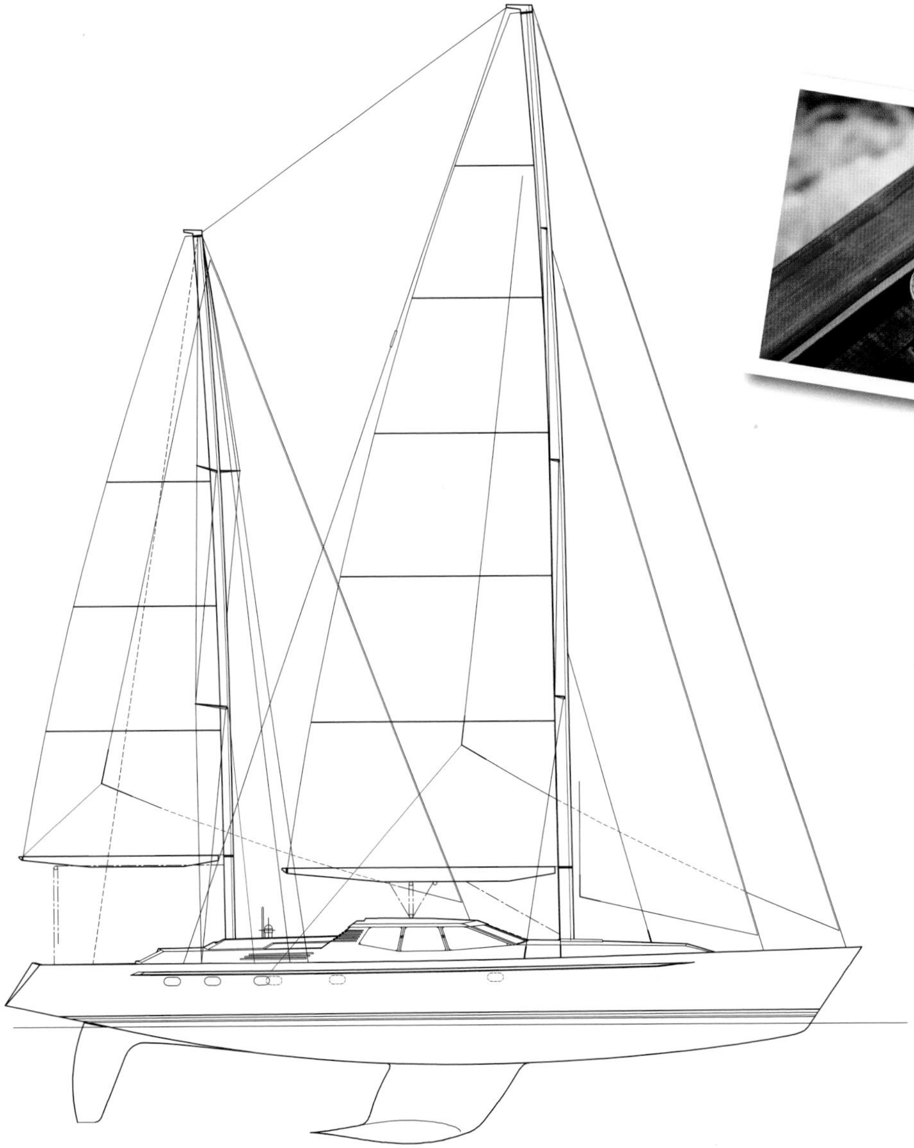

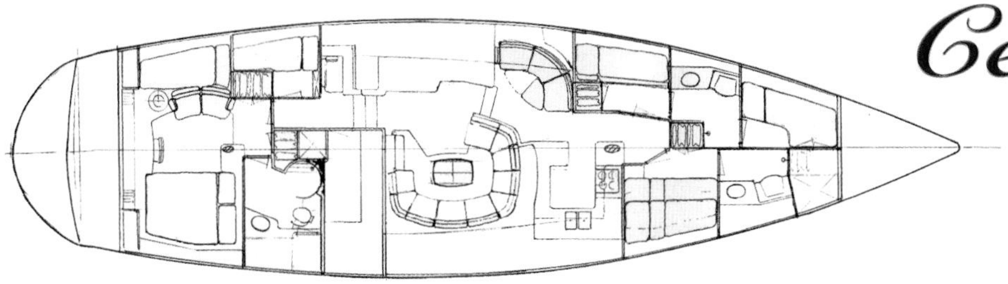

Celtic Spirit
OF FASTNET

Clockwise from top left: Celtic Spirit *after the paint has been stripped from the hull and before respraying.* / *Anchor chain and dynema line layed out and marked in 10 metre lengths – used to tell how much chain has been let out when dropping anchor.* / *The nav station pulled apart during electronic equipment refit.* / Celtic Spirit's *bow before the new decks are fitted.*

The refit

Celtic Spirit of Fastnet returned to Berthons Shipyard in Lymington, England, for her major refit under the expert eye of surveyor John Freeman. Safety was a priority and so the yard was instructed to have the boat commercially rated under MCA. In addition, extensive modifications and replacements were ordered.

To deal with the extreme conditions in Antarctica we would need to change the gas supply from butane to propane, as butane freezes more easily at a lower temperatures. This meant changing all burners and regulators as well. The cooker itself had to be mounted more securely to take the severe pounding expected in the Southern Ocean seas. Next, the bow stem was modified to carry the boats CQR and Bruce anchors, each of which weighed 80 kg. To both anchors 100 m of chain was attached and then a further 100 m of dynema line were added, which has a breaking strain greater than that of the chain. Specially designed rollers for dynema lines were fitted aft which would be used for leading lines ashore while tying up in Antarctica.

Two new fixed blade propellers were manufactured (*Celtic Spirit* has two engines), which we would carry with us, and change in Southern Argentina, before heading across to Antarctica. The two existing folding propellers would have been too delicate to deal with ice particles. A great deal of time was dedicated to working out how we would effect the change over of these propellers, as there are no lift-out facilities that far south and this work would have to be done underwater in icy conditions. There would not be many volunteers for that task! Tools were specially made to allow us to carry out this task. An excellent piece of diving equipment was sourced from the USA, a small, electrically-operated diving compressor, which allows two divers to go down to 10 m under the boat without the normal diving tanks. Our heating and refrigeration systems were replaced and new decks were added. The boat got a new water maker and a complete overhaul of the masts and rigging. We replaced the heavy aluminium spinnaker and whisker poles with lighter carbon ones. The hydraulics were completely overhauled and a new electrical energy management system was installed.

Our radar was upgraded to include ARPA, a system allowing us to identify and track other vessels. As parts and technical support would be virtually impossible to source from Argentina onwards, back up of important equipment was needed as much as possible to avoid carrying excessive spare parts and equipment. The boat carried three compass types: binnacle, fluxgate and our very accurate gyro compass, with both the fluxgate and gyro being available for connection to the radar to support ARPA. Our primary mode of navigation would be using paper charts, however, we had three separate GPS systems independently connected to two navigation systems and a Yeoman plotter for use with our paper charts. We had two sources of weather information, Navtex and a 'moving weather' software programme that downloads weather forecasts via the satellite phone.

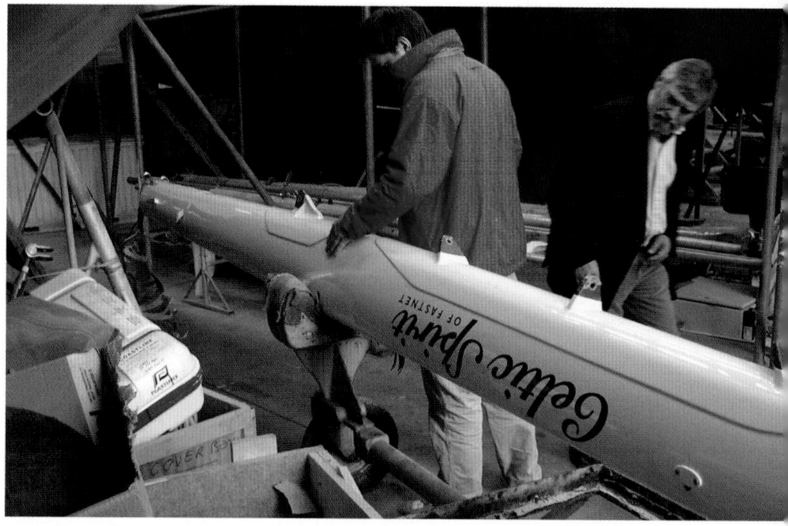

Above: *Ansis and surveyor John Freeman inspect the main boom with new signage.* / ***Below:*** *Bruce and CQR anchors.* / Celtic Spirit *after her respray.*

The crew

In preparing for a voyage it is important to ensure that the boat is seaworthy but it is also necessary to source information, gather charts and pilots books and, most importantly, select crew, without whom the boat would have no reason to go anywhere. On board *Celtic Spirit* each crew member is involved in every aspect of the smooth running of the boat from cooking and cleaning to standing watches and sailing the boat.

Our printed t-shirts said it all – 'Crew wanted for hazardous journey, no pay, very cold, long months of misery assured, a voyage of a lifetime'. This was inspired by Ernest Shackleton's original advertisement seeking crew for *Endurance*. For this Arctic to Antarctic voyage our preference was to minimise crew changes. Ideally, we required a crew who could commit to large sections of the voyage, and get to know *Celtic Spirit's* sailing characteristics. Successful crew would also need to have experience of long ocean voyages as well as a thorough knowledge of emergency routines. Living conditions would be dictated by the weather and the length of passages so the crew would need to work well together over long periods of time during stressful situations. A mixture of age groups was also desirable as some of us were not in the first flushes of youth and we ended up with four very capable crew under the age of thirty who added a bit of agility to our crew mix. We had a great response to our enquiries and chose thirteen crew altogether, however, only eight would sail at any one time with the others joining the boat at different stages of the voyage. The crew represented Ireland, Britain, Latvia, South Africa, Holland, Sweden, Brazil and New Zealand. Eleven languages were spoken fluently between us all and, as it turned out, four of them were accomplished musicians, providing *Celtic Spirit* with its own band. In all, they were a harmonious, fun-loving, interesting and extremely dedicated crew who were the focus of attention wherever we dropped a hook.

Michael Holland

Owner and Skipper
Nationality: *Irish*
Occupation: *Entrepeneur*
Most likely to:
- say 'We will be leaving at 4 a.m.'
- be found at the nav station

Far left, left and above: *Ansis drops the sails. / Grinding the sails in. / Vera plots our position.*

Ansis Dimiters

First Mate and Second Skipper
Nationality: *Latvian*
Occupation: *Sailor*
Most likely to:
- say 'Very good, very good.'
- eat all the chocolates on board

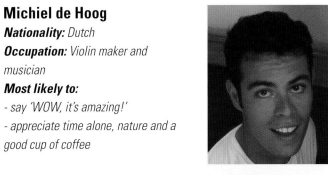

Janet King

Nationality: *South African*
Occupation: *Graphic designer, artist*
Most likely to:
- say 'Very, very beautiful.'
- be found policing the galley

John Petersson (JohnJohn)

Nationality: *Swedish*
Occupation: *Sailor*
Most likely to:
- eat two helpings of food
- be found singing Swedish anthems loudly whilst helming

Blayney Rice

Nationality: *Irish*
Occupation: *Businessman*
Most likely to:
- say 'Are we there yet?'
- make spaghetti bolognese for dinner

Michiel de Hoog

Nationality: *Dutch*
Occupation: *Violin maker and musician*
Most likely to:
- say 'WOW, it's amazing!'
- appreciate time alone, nature and a good cup of coffee

Denis O'Sullivan

Nationality: *Irish*
Occupation: *Builder/developer*
Most likely to:
- get on quietly with the task at hand
- talk about his days working on the oil rigs

Vera O'Herlihy

Nationality: *Irish*
Occupation: *Retired physical education teacher*
Most likely to:
- say 'It was fabulous.'
- sing 'The Harp That Once'

Tineke Berthelson

Nationality: *New Zealander*
Occupation: *Student*
Most likely to:
- say 'I will teach you how to speak English properly.'
- be found reading her book lying on the dinghy

Fabrizio Limena

Nationality: *Brazilian*
Occupation: *Business consultant*
Most likely to:
- say 'What was it like in the last war, Blayney?'
- play 'Hit The Road, Jack' on his saxophone

Igor Mestriner

Nationality: *Brazilian*
Occupation: *Sailor*
Most likely to:
- say 'Indeed!'
- give thanks before eating a meal

Jon Wright

Nationality: *English*
Occupation: *Software designer*
Most likely to:
- prepare the tastiest meals
- take excellent photos

Enda O'Driscoll

Nationality: *Irish*
Occupation: *Systems manager*
Most likely to:
- sort out the computer when it is playing up
- find a lift to a late opening bar in a remote part of Ireland on short notice

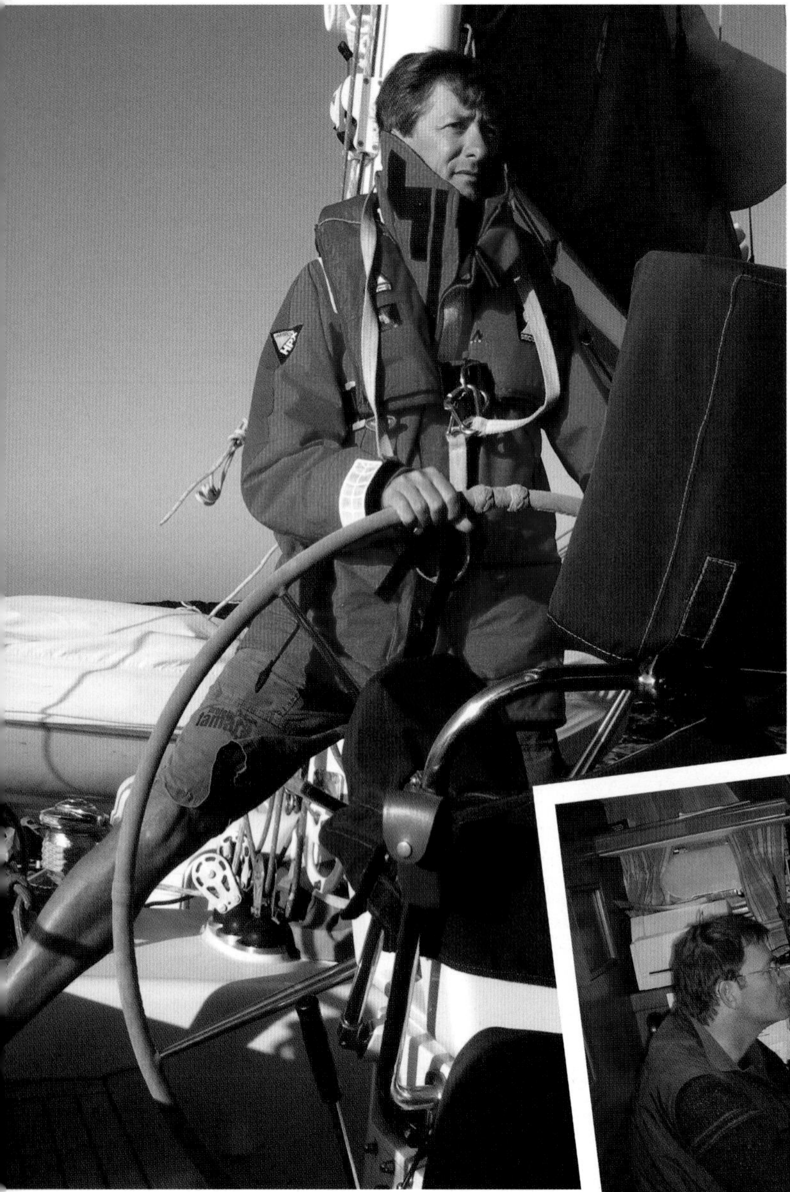

Above and right: *Michael the skipper helms the boat. / Enda checks the radar and course in the nav station.*

A typical day for a crew member

Midnight. Janet has spent fifteen minutes preparing for the watch before her, which involves dressing in appropriate clothing for the conditions at hand and being briefed by the previous watch on hand-over. With any luck, she also gets a cup of tea. This particular watch extends to 3 a.m. and is known as the graveyard watch. It will be shared by one other crew person. At this time all other crew are likely to be below asleep. On watch crew are expected to take full command of the boat. This involves trimming sails and reefing when necessary, updating the log, keeping a look out, taking appropriate action with shipping traffic, watching out for weather predictions and maintaining maximum sailing speed in the right direction. As it is night-time, harnesses must be worn at all times while on deck. The chances of recovering a person from overboard are greatly diminished in darkness, particularly in poor weather. Janet takes turns on the helm, which at night in particular takes a lot of concentration, as sailing will be by compass and 'wind feel'. Frequent shifts in the wind are to be expected especially in the tropics when squalls arise frequently and can cause a shift in wind direction by as much as 40 degrees while the wind can, at the same time, suddenly increase to gale force. In the cold Southern Ocean many layers of clothing are worn in an effort to keep warm and dry. Sometimes it is necessary to go forward on deck to reef the mainsail and this expends a large amount of energy as the motion of the boat in big seas necessitates holding on tightly to avoid losing balance or falling overboard. Waves of freezing water wash down the deck and often a crew person will be waist deep in this fast moving torrent of water while working as fast as possible to complete the task with freezing hands and increasing exhaustion. If the weather is particularly bad, the rule is that the crew next due on watch can be woken up to assist in the task at hand. All crew particularly dislike it when it is raining as both visibility and comfort rapidly deteriorate. At 0245 Janet goes below to wake up the crew who will take over the next watch from 0300 to 0600. When they are ready this new watch crew will be briefed as to expected weather, navigation and any other relevant information.

0330: after a cup of tea and examining the watch rota, Janet collapses, exhausted and cold, into her bunk. She knows that although she is also on lunch duty at 1300, she will have to work in the galley for some time before this and she will also need to find the time to update the boat's website. She shares this task with the skipper but she takes care of it most of the time. Twice a week is laundry day and this task can take some time particularly in heavy seas. Sunday is one of the two days a week allocated for showers and in her spare time Janet will have a very spartan shower. Water conservation on board is vital if the supplies are to last eight people for up to three weeks at a time.

Janet decides that today's lunch will consist of a chicken salad preceded by potato and leek soup. In the heaving galley, lunch can take some time to prepare and being on lunch or dinner duty is one of the dreaded chores on board. It is not easy to stand over a violently moving cooker with four rings in use especially when the contents of a cupboard want to leap out every time one opens its door. The floor can be wet and slippery and it can be unbearably hot. Crew use a huge amount of energy each day so while it may take hours to prepare a meal it is usually devoured in mere minutes in total silence. Luckily, the task of washing up after lunch or dinner duty and making sure that the galley is left in pristine condition is always allocated to a different watch crew. Today is Blayney's turn for the wash-up and he must be careful to minimise the use of water as usual. There is a small leak in the skylight above the galley and, frequently, water pours down on him. The occasional expletive can be heard while others have an amusing laugh at his situation knowing that their fate will come about another time.

1500: after lunch Janet and her co-helper take a break to maintain personal logs and to read. Around her, other crew are busy at their tasks. Today, the daily turn of cleaning the boat's interior falls to the skipper. This involves hoovering and washing floors, and keeping the common areas free of clutter. Each crew is responsible for keeping their assigned heads (toilets) clean. Today JohnJohn is responsible for the exterior cleaning, particularly the cockpit area as this is occupied twenty-four hours a day by crew who sometimes eat there while on watch. Ansis is busy on repair duty as our fridge has stopped working due to an air blockage in the system. He is assisted in this task by the skipper.

On deck Michiel and Igor are having an invigorating sail as the boat is on a broad reach in 25 knots of wind. All sails are flying with reefs in the main and mizzen. We are sailing at 9 knots in moderate seas on a starboard tack.

At 1700 Janet decides to get another two hours' sleep before dinner, which tonight is being prepared by Jon and Fabrizio. We are all happy about this as Jon is considered to be one of the better cooks on board.

After a delicious dinner of dorade (freshly caught yesterday) Janet has just enough time to check her emails, and write to family and friends before she prepares for her next three-hour watch, which begins at 2100. The winds are expected to increase from the northeast so it is likely to be a lively watch. The on-board band decide to have a practice session this evening, Michiel is on mandolin, Fabrizio on saxophone and JohnJohn has his guitar while Igor plays Brazilian drums. Life on board is well and truly settled down with a well-matched team working towards the same fulfilling goal of reaching Antarctica. Tomorrow will be a similarly busy day and our next port of call is more than two weeks away.

Clockwise from top left: *JohnJohn takes a break from the rigours of sailing. / Michiel, Michael the skipper and Denis study charts. / Jon organising dinner in the galley.*

Ireland to Iceland

In June 2005* Celtic Spirit *set sail from Bangor Marina in Northern Ireland to Isafjordur on the northwest corner of Iceland. From there we sailed over the Arctic Circle and to Reykjavik, Iceland's capital. This was planned to be a shake-down sail for the far longer journey to Antarctica that lay ahead of us.

13/06/05

At the ungodly hour of 0330 this morning the crew of *Celtic Spirit* were forced from their bunks, into their wet gear and up on deck. With 20 knots wind abeam we sprung from the pontoon in Bangor Marina, Northern Ireland and made our way out into the wild open sea and 34 knots of breeze from the north. Water sluiced down the decks as *Celtic Spirit* sunk her bow into the oncoming waves. Snorkels and flippers would have been appropriate for the amount of green water we are experiencing. Under mizzen but with both engines, we were still making slow progress against the lumpy sea and strong headwinds.

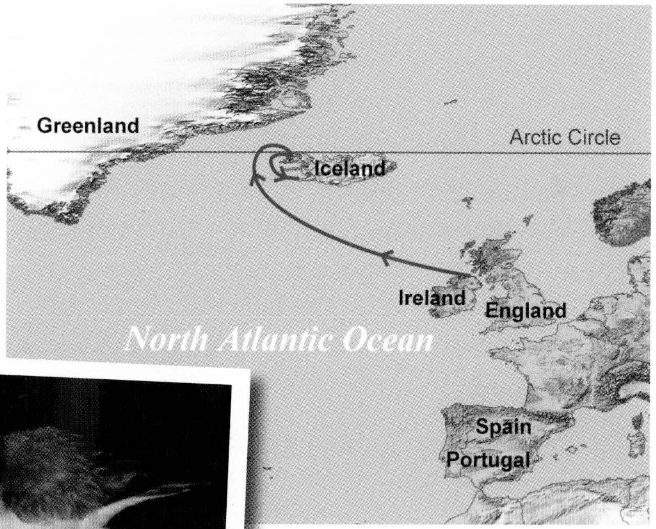

By midday the aft bilge alarm is going off non-stop, our depth sounder is reading less than 2 m and the windlass switches keep setting off the hydraulic pump so we have to switch it off. Meanwhile on the bow, the rings have slipped from the anchor claws. This means the anchor is now loose and needs securing. Ansis goes forward to sort it out and in the process is hit by a large wave, which causes his lifejacket to inflate. Everyone naps on and off as their bodies get used to life aboard and some manage a little soup and bread. Ansis does not feel well but bravely says he 'can manage a small piece of chocolate'! At 1430 a violent clunking noise is heard. The large pin at the foot of the mizzen vang has come out and the mizzen is flailing around uncontrollably. In a hurry we locate the pin, which thankfully is still on board, place it back and glue the nut at the exposed thread end. It is 688 miles to go to the southwest tip of Iceland and we have had our fair share of teething problems for one day.

14/06/05

Today the gale abates and as the wind dies down the sea state becomes calmer. Under these conditions the skipper and Ansis are able to let down the transom and check the bilges where the alarm had been going off throughout yesterday. They remove the water and change the aft bilge pump, which is shot.

Opposite page: *The snow-capped peaks of southwest Iceland: land of fire and ice.* /
Left and above: *Ansis on the foredeck securing the anchor.* / *Ansis with his lifejacket inflated.* /
Right: *Lucky goes for a walk down below.*

At approximately 1700 a small bird lands on deck, exhausted. He tries flying but only makes it forward a little. Then he flies off around in a circle and back into the rigging of the boat, knocking himself out cold. He lands on his back just as a wave sweeps over the deck and carries him aft. He surely would have been swept overboard but for Blayney who scoops him up, rescuing him. We bring him in to the shelter of the cockpit and name him 'Lucky'. We try feeding him bread, biscuit, apple and water but he is not interested. He tries to fly off but is too weak so we bring him into the saloon where it is warmer and place him under the lamp. Bets are on as to Lucky's chances of survival.

Lucky took a fancy to navigation and can now be found under the chart table. Still alive at 3 a.m.!

Blayney's logbook entry

15/06/05

Even though the wind has died down to under 20 knots, it is still from the northeast and big rollers come across us, washing over the boat and into the cockpit. Ansis is keeping a watchful eye on Lucky but eventually falls asleep and does not notice that Lucky is no longer

Clockwise from top left: Celtic Spirit *slows down to allow a container ship on a collision course with us to pass well ahead.* / *Ansis captures the delivery of bread on camera.* / *Janet whisks hot loaves of bread from the oven.* / *Ansis nurses a very poorly Lucky.* / *Danger, Janet in the galley!* / *Jon takes a photo.*

Clockwise from top left: *Enda raises the Icelandic flag. / Land Ahoy! Ansis strikes a pose. / The coastline of Iceland comes into view. / Are we there yet? Janet studies the chart.*

standing. He is so weak he has keeled over but is still alive. On the skipper's suggestion we find a large syringe and Ansis tries to feed him water but it is no use and brave Lucky passes away. Time of death 0930 BST. He is given a suitable burial at sea.

The wind begins to change direction and slacken. We put up the main to supplement the mizzen. Dolphins are spotted behind the boat around 1230.

16/06/05

The nights are getting shorter now and this morning it gets dark around 0100 for about an hour when the first rays of light begins to appear as fine drizzle fills the cockpit. At 0300 a blip is picked up on the radar. Out on deck the lights of a vessel are spotted to starboard. Ten minutes later a check on the radar shows that the vessel is bearing down on us on a definite collision course! We have to slow the boat down, which allows the tanker to pass well ahead of us.

Today for the first time bread is baked, filling the boat with a warm homely smell. As Janet removes the loaves from the oven five pairs of eyes peer over into the galley and photograph this momentous occasion. It does not take them long to devour the fresh bread along with pâté, cheese, ham and jam. It is a fantastic, beautiful day with sunshine and flat seas. Everyone takes advantage by spending time out on deck. The skipper agrees that everyone can have a shower and a few of us wash clothes, which we hang out on the mizzen sheet under the mizzen boom to dry. Later, as we sit eating dinner in the saloon, Blayney spots dolphins swimming alongside the boat. At midnight it is still light.

17/06/05

All sails are out and engines are off. Blue skies stretch out ahead and a few clouds hang on the horizon. The weather is so glorious the crew sit out on deck in t-shirts. It is 95 miles to Iceland's southwest tip. While Michael the skipper is checking charts and working at the nav station he sees two blips on the radar. There is something on the horizon, something that looks like big square blocks. When Enda awakes we tell him we have seen land. He is sceptical and says it is just a cloud. He takes up a gin and tonic seat on the aft deck opposite Blayney and it's not long before he also spots land. Looking through binoculars we see it is definitely a landmass. Enda discovers coverage on his mobile. Everyone is out on deck with their phones, picking up and sending messages. In celebration of sighting land we have a little wine with our dinner.

Ansis reads from the *Rough Guide to Iceland* from the section on translations. Apparently the Icelandic insult each other with the phrases 'you cod' or 'you are not worth many fish'. The latter soon becomes a much-used phrase among the crew.

18/06/05

The wind is up and the boat is heeled right over. We still have no wind instruments due to a power failure caused by the hydraulic windlass so at a guess there must be 25 to 30 knots of breeze. Taking the boat off auto helm and turning her into the wind we put two reefs in the main sail and mizzen. We plot our position every hour on the chart and check the radar regularly.

The scenery is spectacular as we leave behind a huge peak topped with ice and head towards the next peninsula, passing the bay where there is apparently good whale watching. Unfortunately we encounter no whales. Slowly the wind and sea state decrease, which allows us to take out a full headsail.

Throughout the day the wind dies further and so our boat speed is much reduced. We had estimated roughly twelve and a half hours to Isafjordur. It will now take us longer. This inspires much plotting and estimating of time. Our skipper begins to alter course to close in on the coastline and decides we must make it in before bar closing times. He puts a call in to Isafjordur on VHF. Isafjordur is the capital of the west fjords region and has 4,000 inhabitants. It is set in a fjord with steep mountains on either side, a natural harbour and is traditionally a fishing port.

Left: *(top) Reefing the main. | (middle) Dropping the sails as we make our way into Isafjordur. | (bottom) Michael our skipper contacts the authorities in Isafjordur by VHF.*
Right: *(top and bottom) The dramatic coastline as we approach Isafjordur.*

Top: *The crew before we leave the boat to explore Isafjordur (left to right): Ansis, Michael, Janet, Blayney, Enda and Jon.* ***Above, left and right:*** *Local people from Isafjordur on board* Celtic Spirit *for a party.*

By 2230 we are tied up on the outer western pier. Waiting to greet us is the harbour master and police customs. The harbour master is eager to greet us and tells us that there is an Irish night in the next village while handing us brochures on Isafjordur. Two officials come aboard where we fill out customs forms and have our passports stamped. We have to count bottles of wine and the excess of the allowed amount is sealed and locked away.

We walk over to the town and find a bar and restaurant, Pizza 67, where there is live music. We spend the evening here enjoying the atmosphere and at closing time the skipper orders Ansis and Jon to invite everyone in the place back to the boat for a party. As the night goes on, people arrive and leave as word filters through the town that a boat is in port with a party on board. There is much singing and dancing and as there is no darkness at night here no one realises that it is actually morning!

19/06/05

After our very late night, the crew slept until the afternoon. Ansis made us a breakfast of egg, cauliflower, tomato, cucumber, cheese, yoghurt, chocolate biscuits and chocolate. Is this a typical Latvian meal? Ansis also organises a taxi to hot pools (geysers) which we have been told are in the next village. The taxi ride takes us through a huge tunnel that seems to go on forever but we all get a surprise when the cab driver takes a right at the junction in the middle of the tunnel! Yes, a tunnel with a junction. Completed in 1995 this tunnel links Isafjordur to the towns of Sudureyri, Flateyri and Pingeyri.

We arrive at the village of Sudureyri where it is cold and drizzly. The baths we have come to visit consist of one large swimming pool and four small Jacuzzi type pools and a sauna all set outdoors. We find the large swimming pool not particularly warm but one by one we make our way through the small pools, each one hotter than the next. We order coffee, which is served to us in flasks at the pool side as mist pours over the mountain that looms overhead. We wonder if the Blue Lagoon will be able to beat this!

Everyone falls asleep in the taxi as we head back to Isafjordur and Pizza 67 for food. While we are there we are joined by some of the friends we made the night before. More beer and *craic* follows. We ask for a typical Icelandic drink and Ragnar gets us Iceland's speciality Brennivin, or Black Death, a clear shot that can be drunk as a beer chaser. It is schnapps made from fermented pulp and flavoured with caraway seeds and has a high alcohol content, 37.5%. At closing time we head back to the boat and watch the video of the party we had the night before. More drink and dancing follows until it is 0400 and time to leave. Casting off we wave our new friends goodbye.

We'd just left Isafjordur at 4 a.m. after a weekend full of fun and new friends. Everyone was dog-tired from a long weekend. I was feeling wistful, as always when leaving a wonderful place to which I'm unlikely to return. So, not yet ready to sleep, I volunteered for the first watch. The skipper's instructions were perfectly clear as usual 'Sail north until we cross the Arctic Circle and then wake everyone up.' And as I'd come to appreciate from Blayney from the last few days he followed up with a quick-witted 'But don't hit it!' One night before the shortest day of the year, the sun was sleeping behind a blanket of grey, which wrapped itself around the sky from horizon to horizon. Everything took on the same dull muted tones, the sky, sea, light and even the sound of the sea dissolved into the wind. The entire world

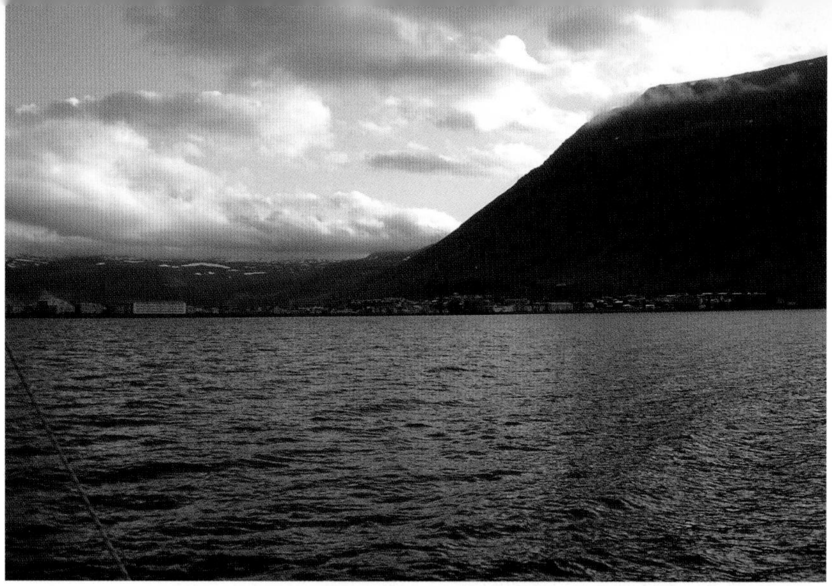

Above: *(top) The sign outside our favourite restaurant Pizza 67. | The crew meet up with our new friends Ragnar and Mia (on the left) in Pizza 67.* ***Right:*** *(top) The town of Isafjordur set below the mountains. | (middle) Seagulls flying with* Celtic Spirit *at the Arctic Circle.*

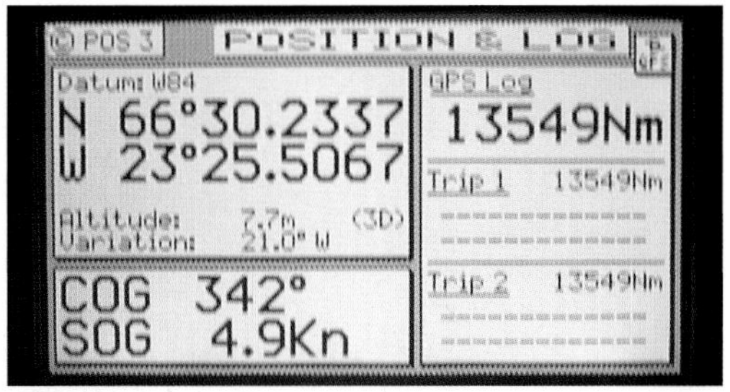

Clockwise from top left: *Celebrating crossing the Arctic Circle (from left): Blayney, Ansis, Michael, Enda, Janet and Jon. / Our GPS reading – proof that we made it! / Blayney points to the Arctic Circle. / Michael opens a bottle of champagne. / What the Arctic Circle really looks like.*

became featureless. I could have believed I was completely alone in the world if it had not been for the company of around fifty sea birds accompanying Celtic Spirit on her journey north. They followed us silently, gliding effortlessly alongside. They didn't seem to be in any hurry or after anything from us, never screeching for food nor resting on board, it seemed just like they were after the company. I was amazed by how close they would glide next to me while I was on the wheel, only an arm's reach away for minutes on end. Finally they broke off, changing direction and heading on alone just before the GPS informed me that we'd reached our destination. A good job too, as only minutes later there would have been champagne corks to dodge as the freshly rested crew, happy to have made it to the Arctic without hitting the circle, cheered in celebration.

Jon Wright's diary entry

20/06/05

The crew are woken for the 'sighting' of the Arctic Circle. It's 1025 and freezing. Everyone on deck hugs each other to the sound of the CD *Music to Watch Girls By*, which inspires dancing on deck. We line up for photos and video. As the boat rolls tripods and cameras fall over. The skipper brings out a bottle of champagne, shakes it and then throws it into the sea. At which Blayney comments, 'What did he just do? What a waste!'

By 1400 there is a constant 20 knots from the northeast. It's raining and foggy but beginning to clear and get cold! By 2000 winds are gusting to 45 knots and the seas are building. We are making good time to Reykjavik. ETA 1100, 22 June 2005, 135 miles to go.

21/06/05

A nice day with reefed headsail and mizzen in 20 knots northeast and the coastline of Reykjavik is in sight. Two dolphins play on our bow wave, giving us a welcome to Reykjavik. We calculate that we are about three hours away from port. As the coast becomes clearer Janet plots our position and is about to wake the skipper when he appears. He calls in to the Port Authorities and then it's time for everyone to get up. All sails come down as we plot our position every half hour then every fifteen minutes, then every ten minutes as we get closer. The skipper is anxious to be plotted on the large-scale chart. We find our way in without any problems and come alongside the visitors' pontoon at 0915. Once *Celtic Spirit* is tied up, we have a large breakfast with eggs, toast, rashers, cereal and yoghurt.

The crew head into town to explore this vibrant, energetic and cosmopolitan capital with its multicoloured houses. Reykjavik is a combination of modern and medieval but it is expensive even by Dublin's standards. Its air is clean and its water is unpolluted.

22/06/05

This morning the skipper got the crew out of bed and organised them to do various jobs. Provisioning lists were written up, water tanks were filled and bilges emptied. It took a few of us to pack the bags of provisions in the supermarket and load them into the waiting cab. When it came time to pay, the guy behind the till said, 'That's the most anyone has spent here.' The skipper, surprised, asks, 'You mean this week?' 'No, ever!' was the reply. It took some time before the credit card system could process the transaction.

While in Reykavik we find an Irish bar called the Celtic Cross and, of course, we must go in for a drink. Our skipper goes exploring, disappearing down a corridor. When he returns he insists that we all follow

Opposite page: *(top) Janet, Michael, Blayney and Jon enjoying the Blue Lagoon. / (bottom left) Jon amongst the steam at the hottest part of the Lagoon. / (bottom right) The pale blue water lies between black volcanic rock.* **This page:** *(clockwise from top left) Enda and Ansis help protect the modesty of a statue. / The coffin in the 'wake room' in the Celtic Cross bar. / Old whale boats in Reykjavik harbour.*

him back down the corridor, which leads into a darkened room. In the centre is a black coffin surrounded by sofas and chairs. There is a stunned silence as we all try to size up the situation. The coffin's main function is now as a table. A rather morbid looking character sits staring down at his drink and the coffin. He looks like he is in mourning. A single candle is burning. The atmosphere is charged and it feels as if we have walked in on something momentous. The skipper encourages us in and so we all take a seat realising we are in the 'wake' room. Our friend who was obviously quite drunk did not seem to mind. In fact he rather seemed to enjoy our company.

23/06/05

We take a trip to the Blue Lagoon Spa which is set in a rocky, volcanic lava field landscape. A pale blue lake with mud waters full of natural minerals, white silica mud, blue green algae and warm geothermal seawater, it ranges in temperature from lukewarm to almost boiling depending on where you are within the pools. Although over-run with tourists we still enjoy soaking up the warm waters, smearing white mud on our faces to take advantage of its healing properties.

Above: *Upward and return crews get together on the deck of* Celtic Spirit. *Back row (from left): Vera, Enda, Janet, Michael, Blayney. Front row (from left): Ansis, Jon and Denis.*

Iceland to Ireland

Our return from Iceland brings us past Rockall to the west coast of Ireland. We visit Frenchport and Castletownbere where we are part of a mayday relay and end our journey from the Arctic in Kinsale on the south coast of Ireland.

Opposite page: Celtic Spirit *tied up in Reykjavik.*
Left and above right: *Ansis tries his hand at fishing. / Fishing hook.*

24/06/05
Our wake-up call comes at 0600. With lines set up we are ready to go and leave the pontoon at 0730, heading out of port, trying to find the leading marks once more. Fenders are brought in, lines are coiled and packed away. We attempt to get the mainsail up but the halyard is caught on the mast light. Janet volunteers and is hoisted up the mast to untangle it. Then we are out into the bay with genoa, main and mizzen up, winds building and engines off, and we change course to head for the end of the peninsula.

At the south-west tip of Iceland we change course, 142 degrees to head for the northwest of Ireland. Winds are now at 20 knots and still building. Head sail comes in and staysail goes out reducing sail area in order to cope with the increase in wind. Everyone is sleepy and trying to catch up on some rest while two dolphins playfully follow us for a while.

25/06/05
Mizzen and headsail are reefed. Winds have built to 27 knots and water is coming through the companion way. Denis, Jon and Janet go forward to put the last remaining reef in the mainsail. Once the reef is in, Jon notices that there is a tear down the main. This means it must be dropped completely or the sail will tear further. It takes all Jon's energy to get the sail down. The wind and seas continue to build. All our gear is now soaked through from our visit to the mast.

The whole day, the wind blows a constant 27 to 30 knots plus, with a big lumpy sea. No one is feeling great and everyone is sleepy. We sit around the saloon watching the seas heaping up through the windows. It is Vera's watch. She makes a dash from her bunk straight to the cockpit. The boat lurches and she falls across to the other side of the cockpit. She is holding on to the sheets of the main track. In her haste to get out on deck she has forgotten her life jacket and harness, which are essential in heavy weather. Janet passes her both and makes sure she clips her harness to life jacket and clipping point in the cockpit. It is now 507 miles to north-west tip of Ireland. ETA 1700 Tuesday 28th.

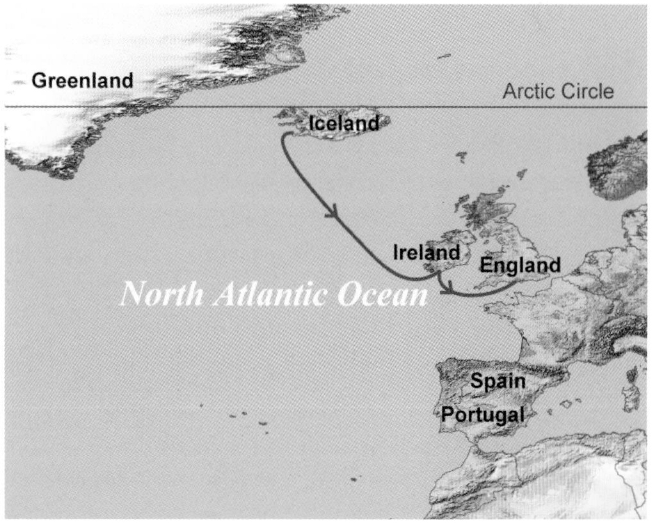

26/06/05

The wind and sea state are now decreasing. Winds are down to 21 knots of breeze. Ansis climbs up onto the boom and stitches a repair into our torn mainsail. Once he has finished we hoist the main when Blayney, at the wheel, accidentally causes the boat to gybe, a dangerous and violent motion.

Our skipper is on the warpath and wants the boat speed kept up! He is thirsty and wants to get to a pub on the west coast of Ireland asap. Blacksod Bay ETA 2000 Tuesday.

During the afternoon the winds decrease. The fog lifts to reveal a pleasant evening in 15 knots. Ansis is fishing. We see a dolphin briefly. Ansis catches nothing as usual and gives up. By 2300 the fog has closed in again and visibility is not good. We are unable to see even a boat length in front of us, which means being extra vigilant on the radar. A blip appears less than 12 miles away. A constant watch is kept on deck and we check on the radar every ten minutes. At 2330 the blip is just over 6 miles away and we are certain it is on a collision course with us although we cannot see it and are relying on the information on the radar. We alter course 10 degrees to starboard in order to avoid collision with the vessel. It passes ahead of us 3 miles away and we return to our correct course. We are sure it is the same vessel on the same route we encountered on the way to Iceland. By 0100 visibility has improved but it is now darker.

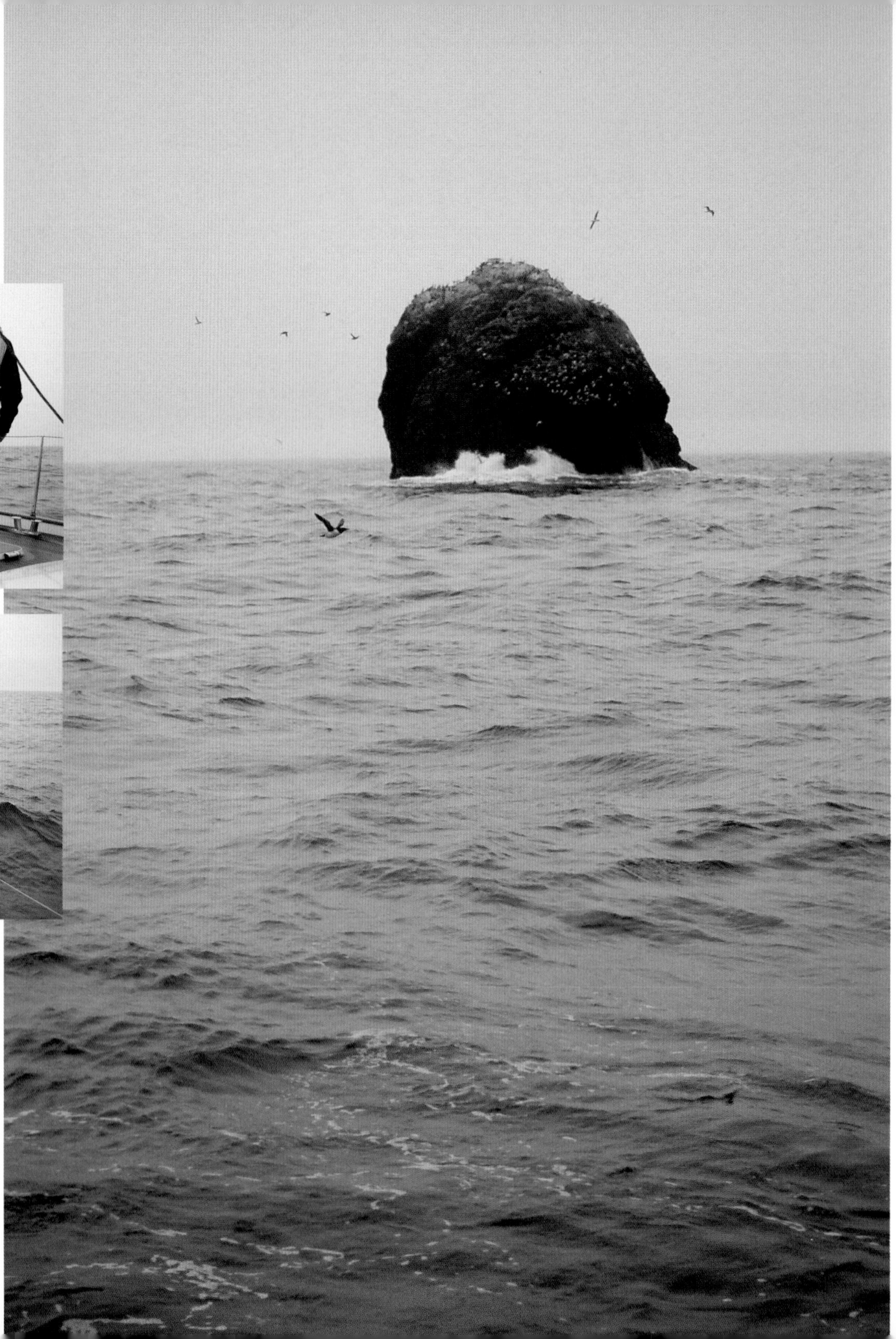

Above *(top and bottom)* ***and right:*** *Janet, Blayney and Vera take photos on the bow with Rockall in the background. / Rockall, inhabited only by birds.*

27/06/05

By 0830 Rockall is abeam of us to port. We turn the boat in order to get closer to it, the cameras come out and we photograph it at length. Rockall is a controversial rock whose ownership is disputed between Ireland and Great Britian. It sticks up in the middle of the Atlantic

Clockwise from far left: *All our sails flying. / Ansis has a snooze on deck. / Jon plays cards. / Ansis and the 'goodie box'. / Chocolate, Ansis' favourite food group. / Denis adjusts the sails. / Vera on dinner duty in the galley. / The skipper reading up information in the pilot book.*

Ocean some 424 km northwest of Donegal, Ireland, a small rocky islet inhabited only by seagulls and puffins. A few seals pop their heads up out of the sea to say hello. We turn the boat back in the direction of Ireland and shake the reefs out of the main. The wind turns light, down to 11 knots and westerly, and, in turn, our boat speed falls below 6 knots. The engines go on, assisted by a full main, mizzen and headsail. Eventually the mist closes in once more which makes a perfect atmosphere for a hot dinner of stew.

28/06/05

This morning brings mist with fine drizzle. As the wind moves around, we are on the other tack switching runners and adjusting sails. The wind increases then drops back down again. The sun makes a brief appearance and then we are back in fog. Denis gets out of bed to see the sun but makes coffee instead. We have biscuits with our coffee up on deck. Vera, Blayney and Michael get up while Ansis goes to bed and Blayney starts thinking about what to make for lunch. Michael wants his computer fixed. He calculates distances to anchoring, Blacksod Bay 72 miles, ETA 2200 or Frenchport 54 miles, ETA 2000. He decides to wake Jon for lunch but really he wants his computer fixed. So Jon has to work for his lunch. Lunch is tasty and Michael gives the order for a tidy up in readiness for our going ashore. Vera is on wash-up duty and Blayney hoovers.

Later everyone is out on deck, chatting. Land is spotted and Blayney decides there is snow on the nearest peak as it has a bright white covering. Skipper comments that it should not be snow as we are further south and the weather should be warmer. On looking through binoculars we can see it is a lighthouse and realise that this is Eagle Island. The coastline draws slowly closer and coverage returns on our mobile phones. Messages start flying back and forth. Ansis puts lasagne on for dinner. From a good distance away the skipper decides to drop the sails. We drop the main, then mizzen and furl in the headsail. Once all the sails are in we realise that the engines are no longer in gear. We are bobbing in the ocean going

Above top to bottom: *Jon in the engine room, ready to relay commands. / Getting the dinghy ready for launching. / The dinghy takes off across the bay.* ***Right top and bottom:*** *Frenchport Bay. / The entrance to Frenchport Bay.*

Clockwise from left: *Denis, Vera, Michael, Janet and Ansis in the dinghy ready to go ashore. / Guinness, a welcome sign. / Ansis, Blayney, Michael, Janet, Jon, Vera and Denis. / Lavelles Eagle Bar in Corclough, north-west Ireland.*

nowhere! It is an electrical problem with the box at the helm. Ansis has to manually engage the engines. We try both and use only one so that we have a back up.

Slowly we edge closer to the bay of Frenchport and begin to distinguish the entrance. Finally we have it and slowly proceed in. Jon and Blayney are dispatched to the anchors, Ansis to the controls in the engine room and Vera and Janet place themselves between the cockpit and companion way so as to relay commands from the skipper on deck to Ansis in the engine room. Visual commands for forward reverse and neutral are given. We arrive into the little bay where a few fishing boats bob happily on their moorings and there is a pier to starboard. Finally the process of dropping the anchors begins. Instructions filter from the helm through Vera and Janet to Ansis in air traffic control fashion and then back again in confirmation. The first attempt fails but all is well on the second.

Once relieved from our duties Vera and Janet pour gin and tonics for all. However, the rest of the crew are all too busy trying to figure out how to dispatch the dinghy. A system of blocks and ropes are set up on the mizzen boom, one for either end of the dinghy. It takes all the men to manoeuvre the dinghy around and into the water. Once it is in, the engine is lowered and tied on but it takes several attempts to start. When the boat goes in for a refit a more efficient launching system for the dinghy will be installed. It will reduce manpower and also reduce the load on the mizzen boom. In the meantime, Vera and Janet have the table set and dinner is served.

After dinner everyone grabs their gear and we are off in two dinghy loads to the beach. We have read up on a bar that is in the vicinity. The directions describe it as 'two miles to the village and past the graveyard'. Denis is convinced that he sees the pub and knows where it is and we set off. It is a long walk over and down the hill then up the other side and we turn right at the next road junction. Still no bar or graveyard so Vera knocks on the door of a house to ask directions and she is told to 'carry on up the hill to the top where the cluster of buildings and lights are'. We walk at a marathon pace to get there before closing time finally arriving at the lit Guinness sign. Venturing in we find it is a large bar which is mostly empty apart from a few regulars sitting at the counter. There is a big aerial photo of Eagle Island over the fireplace. We have a total of four rounds of drinks, peanuts and a jolly good laugh. At last orders (a double round) we asked for a cab to get us back to the dinghy, which they happily organised for us and which arrived promptly at closing time. Our cab driver was glad to take a group picture of us outside the pub, Lavelles Eagle Bar. Then he drove us back down to our dinghy on the beach and refused to take payment. He had never driven people who had arrived in their humble town straight from Iceland!

29/06/05

After a late start we head out of Frenchport Bay at 1500 under engine, mizzen and genoa as there is little wind. This evening we watch the most beautiful sunset over the Atlantic, blue skies tinged with scattered soft pink clouds.

30/06/05

We pass Slynehead at 0030. The wind is still light and variable. We are heading to Castletownbere 120 miles away, on the south coast, ETA 1930. Through the early hours of the morning the wind increases to 36 knots but by 0900 has dropped back down dramatically to 13 knots and we are back under engine. By 1100 we are approaching the Blasket Islands in a big rolling sea and some sunshine. At 1630 we are 4 miles southeast of Dursey Head with all our sails up. We drop anchor in Castletownbere at 1930 and head ashore to McCarthy's Bar.

Clockwise from top right: *A pastel sky. / We pass the Skellig Islands: Blayney, Ansis, Janet, Michael, Vera and Denis in front of Little Skellig. / Skellig Michael*

01/07/05

We stow the dinghy and raise the anchor. It is 1030, miserable and raining. Heading past Beare Island and at the mouth of Castletownbere entrance, Denis spots what he at first thinks is a kayaker. On closer inspection, he realises that it is not a person in a kayak but is, in fact, someone in a small white open motor launch frantically waving a bright orange life jacket. It is difficult to see him as he frequently disappears behind the waves of a big swell. He is dangerously close to the rocks and has no means of communication. He has an anchor down but with no engine and the strong swell this may not hold for long and he will most likely be dashed on the sharp rocks in the shadow of Beare Island. We send out a mayday relay and stand by while Bantry Radio call out Castletownbere Lifeboat. It is not long before it speeds out of Castletownbere stopping near to the motor launch. It does not take them long to skilfully get the frightened man aboard. They contact us and thank us for our help and we leave the scene at 1130. *Celtic Spirit* heads for Kinsale and the end of the Arctic part of this journey.

Clockwise from top left: *The lighthouse on Beare island. / Castletownbere lifeboat at anchor. / The town of Castletownbere. / Michael, Ansis, Denis and Blayney perfect the dinghy launch.*

England to Spain

During the summer of 2006,* Celtic Spirit *began her long voyage south starting in Lymington on the south coast of England, sailing down past the Bay of Biscay to northwest Spain and in short legs covering its north-west coast. Galicia is the poorest province in Spain but it is beautiful, green and inexpensive.

Opposite page: *Passing the Needles in poor visibility.* | **Above:** *Last-minute bow modifications being put to the test in Lymington.* | **Right:** *Strong winds and a lumpy sea at the start our sail south.*

27/05/06

After months of preparation, the refit is complete. We spend a few tense days sorting out the last-minute issues and then finally, *Celtic Spirit* and her crew are ready to go. Scores of shopping bags are loaded on to the boat and stowed away, 1,500 litres of diesel is taken on board and the water tanks are filled.

At 1245 we depart Lymington marina and make our way into the Solent, passing the Needles in poor visibility and 25 knots from the west, which soon increases to 30 knots. With 500 miles to go to our next stop, we are on our way south!

28/05/06

The sun has edged its way through a grey blanket of cloud casting a warm sparkle on the sea and giving a promising start to the day!

Michiel's logbook entry

29/05/06

Early this morning a swallow-type bird lands on deck briefly, looking very tired. He flies away an hour later. We are sailing goose winged with poled-out genny and mizzen. The sun is out and it's a lovely day but cold. This evening we have three pigeons on board. One arrived this afternoon and was fed and watered. Then another landed and then another. We notice that they are ringed and from Portugal so they must be racing pigeons hitching a ride!

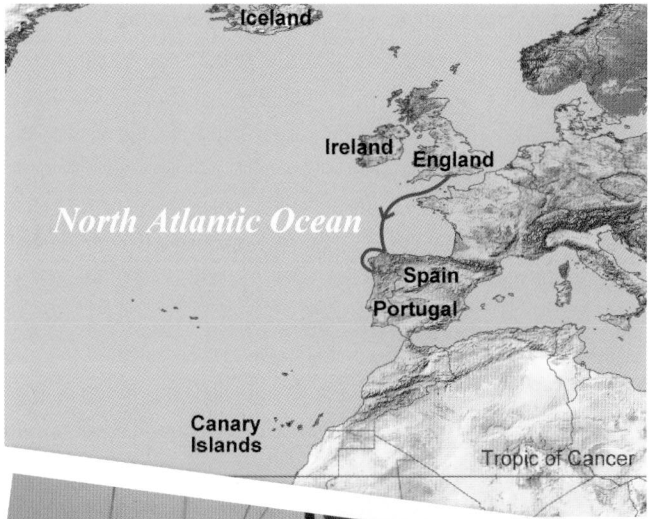

30/05/06
It's a beautiful starry night sailing in 20 knots of wind. We are heading to Ria de Cedeira in Galicia on the north-west coast of Spain. The wind is building and going east. Our three pigeons eat breakfast and happily wander about the cockpit where they are making a mess on the floor. The wind picks up to 33 knots. Our three hitchhikers, now named Bird Flu, One Flew Over the Cuckoo's Nest and Gimble, have dined on a lunch of bread and lettuce but declined the tomato and onion. Land is now clearly in sight. While the crew marvel at the sight of approaching land our guests take off in unison and are soon gone from view. We drop anchor in a small bay just north of the breakwater at Ria de Cedeira. It's a beautiful anchorage but the wind is very strong, up to 35 knots. The town is very quiet although we manage to find a bar with some lively characters who chat with us and take us to a family-run restaurant. We are their only customers but we eat well and they are delighted to have us.

31/05/06
This afternoon we weigh anchor in strong winds and in the process damage the chain strop. We set off in 35 knots and over the afternoon the winds reach 39 knots and the sea builds up in accordance. At 1830 we drop anchor in 8 m of water in Ares. Michiel finds us a lovely place to have a meal, O'Bodegón. There is a bar there and after our meal we stay for a drink. The owners are very friendly and we have such a good time that they let us stay for hours having locked up the premises.

01/06/06
After exploring the town of Ares, taking a swim and walking on the beaches, we sail to La Coruna in pleasant 27 knots from the northeast. On our way into La Coruna harbour we are boarded by customs officers who check the boat's papers and passports. They stay on board until we berth. They are very friendly and courteous.

La Coruna is a superb old Galician city thought to be first settled by people of Celtic origin. Picasso spent four years living and studying here when he was young. We sit sipping our *café con leche* in cafés on the edge of the Plaza de Maria Pita, which is overlooked by the

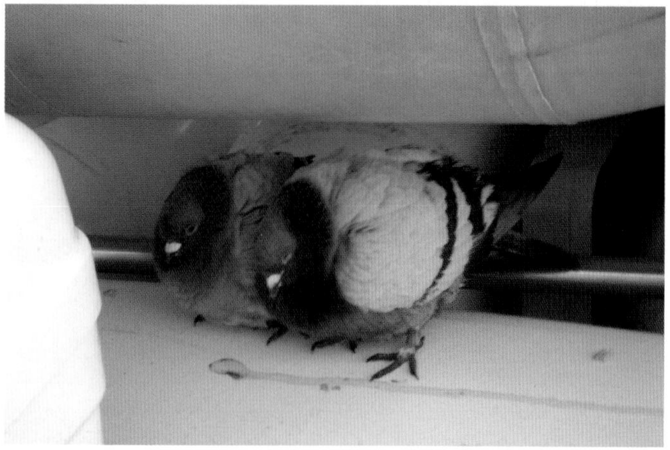

Top: *Poled-out genny for down-wind sailing.* | ***Bottom:*** *Our hitchhikers, (left) Gimble, (right) Bird Flu and One flew Over the Cuckoo's Nest.*

Clockwise from top left: *Direction and wind-speed instruments – it's blowing a gale!* | *Our first sight of land as we arrive in Spain.* | *Gin and tonics and snacks on arrival at anchorage – a* Celtic Spirit *tradition.* | *The green coast of Galicia.*

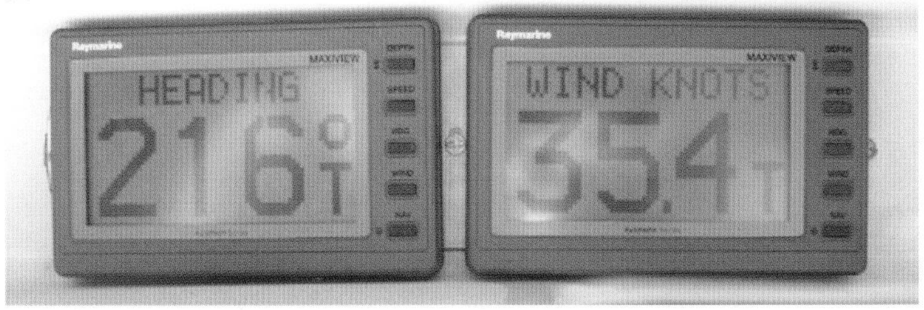

Above: *(top) Ria de Cedeira as seen by Michiel from the cockpit of* Celtic Spirit. */ (bottom) The evening light catches the shoreline in Ria de Cedeira. /* ***Right:*** *The view of the town from the bridge, Ria de Cedeira.*

Above: *(top) Ansis, Vera and Denis with the dinghy – our means of transport ashore. / (middle) O'Bodegón Ria Ares: Ansis, Blayney and Michael deep in conversation. / (bottom) Blayney performs his rendition of 'Fields of Athenry' for the owner of O'Bodegón, Michiel and Michael.*

impressive Municipal Palace and at night we eat in any one of the many tapas bars on the streets that lead into the square. Rich in history, the Old City is full of beautiful churches, squares and gardens. A cycle, walk or tram ride brings you along the coastline to Torres de Hercules (The Tower of Hercules), the world's oldest lighthouse still in operation and steeped in legend.

28/06/06

Almost a month passes before crew return to the boat in La Coruna. After the usual provisioning and stowing we get a weather forecast and leave at 1530. There is not much wind and by 2030 we have dropped anchor in Laye Bay in a slight swell and light breeze. We head ashore and walk along the promenade looking for somewhere to eat. Just outside a modern-looking bar, some people are barbecuing sardines. We go in and order beer and before long we are being brought fresh barbecued sardines and bread. We eat heartily and the sardines are very tasty, especially when washed down with plenty of beer. We are quite surprised that the bill comes to only €20.82 for a whole evening of eating and drinking.

29/06/06

Today's sail starts at 1230 with little wind and under engine but by 1700 the wind has picked up to 30 knots from the northwest. The sun beats down as we arrive into the beautiful, well-sheltered bay of Ria de Muros where there is plenty of space to moor. We tie the dinghy up in the fishing harbour amongst the many fishing boats and make our way over to an area where two large stages are erected. There is a live music performance and crowds of people are dancing. A carnival atmosphere fills the streets and a spectacular fireworks display sets the sky ablaze. This is the feast of San Pedro, the patron saint of Muros, the biggest annual festival to be held here.

Clockwise from top left: *Vera and Denis listen to Michael tell a story. / Michiel says how much he is enjoying the sailing. / Ansis playing barman in O'Bodegón. / Colourful boats on the slip at Ria Ares. / The peaceful calm of Ria Ares.*

30/06/06

This morning we take the dinghy back over to Muros for coffee and croissants and find the best place is directly across the road from the harbour. The narrow streets that snake through the centre of town are filled with market stalls selling everything from bread and cheese, fruit and vegetables to plenty of very inexpensive clothing. This outdoor market is held weekly and we take advantage by buying a few provisions. From there we walk along the attractive promenade that runs from the harbour along the length of the town's sea front. The residential part of Muros stretches up the steep slope behind the town centre and promenade. Steps, pathways and narrow roads lead up the hillside. We venture into a place called the Captains Bar for more coffee, which we chase with a few shots. The afternoon is spent

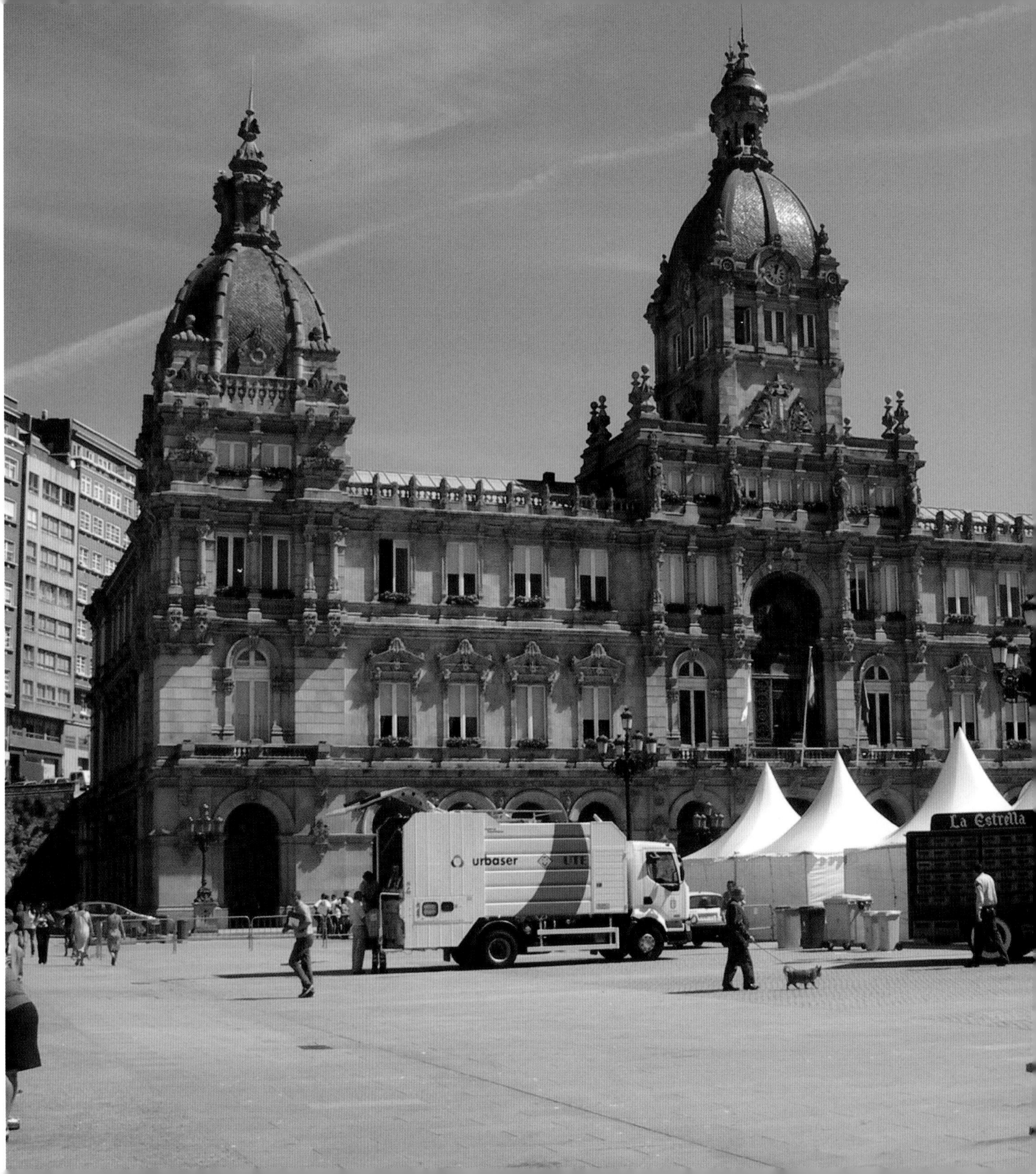

Opposite page: *(left) Torres de Hercules, the oldest working lighthouse in the world. / (right) Plaza de Maria Pita and the Municipal Palace.*
Above: *(top) Picturesque Laye Bay. / (left) The remains of sardines and beer. / (right) Blayney, Ansis and Michael enjoying an inexpensive night out in Laxe.*

Clockwise from top left: *The fishing harbour at Muros. / Fireworks light up the sky. / The Promenade. / Blayney, Michael and Ansis at the Captains Bar. / Ansis up the mast doing repairs. / A heat haze over the bay in Muros. / The narrow streets of Muros.*

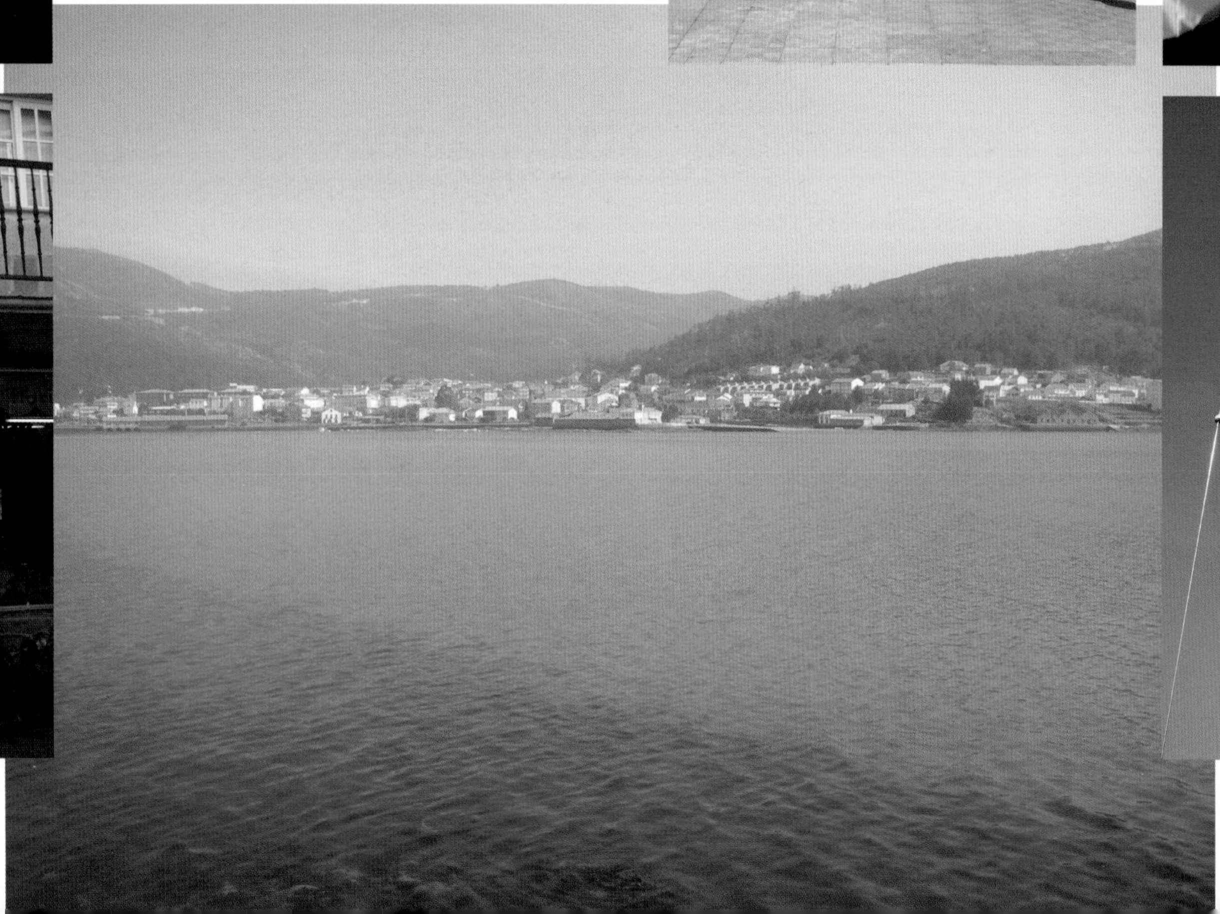

cleaning the hull of the boat and doing various maintenance chores. We decide to have dinner on board this evening.

01/07/06

Today's journey takes us to Cambados on the south-east entrance of Ria Arosa in the Pontevedra province. According to the pilot the entrance is complicated and on the charts the passage looks difficult but we find it is more straightforward in practice. We arrive at 1700 and are anchored by 1930, surrounded by fish farms about 3 or 4 miles out. We take the dinghy into a small harbour and tie to a pontoon. Cambados is an old Galician town full of granite buildings along narrow streets. It is very quiet with few people around. We find a great restaurant of Michelin-Star standard upstairs over a bar, Yayo Daporta. Here we sample bottles of wine from their vast selection. This part of Pontevedra is the centre of wine production in this region and is best known for its Albarino, which we wholeheartedly enjoy. It is clear when we leave that nothing opens until after 2300 and by 0100 the town now resembles the Temple Bar district in Dublin. The streets are alive and buzzing with people spilling out of bars everywhere.

Top: *(from left to right) Ansis, Janet and Blayney take a dinghy ride ashore. / Entertainment in the square. /* ***Left:*** *The streets of Cambados.*

On the corner of the square a bar, Brothers, is holding a promotional evening for a new brand of gin called Bombay Dry Gin. Each purchase receives a scratch card and we clean up with prizes. Outside in the square there are plenty of scantily-clad girls and boys, fire juggling, dancing and adding to the party atmosphere.

02/07/06

We leave at lunchtime in little wind, no sun and heavy fog. The poor visibility makes our departure difficult, especially with all the fishing boats all around us. We decide on a quick stop before heading onward to Bayona and anchor at Isla Ons around 1500. Heading up the hill we pass a little church and find a shack above the beach where we sit down and have a beer. Everyone has a siesta! We leave this little island at 1730 and arrive in the marina in Bayona at 2000. It is a beautiful town and *Celtic Spirit's* home for the next few weeks.

Clockwise from top left: *The view from the bar in Isla Ons. / Blayney goes to the church on the hill, Isla Ons. / Michael and Blayney have a siesta after a couple of beers while Janet looks on in amusement. / Ansis, the sleeping beauty.*

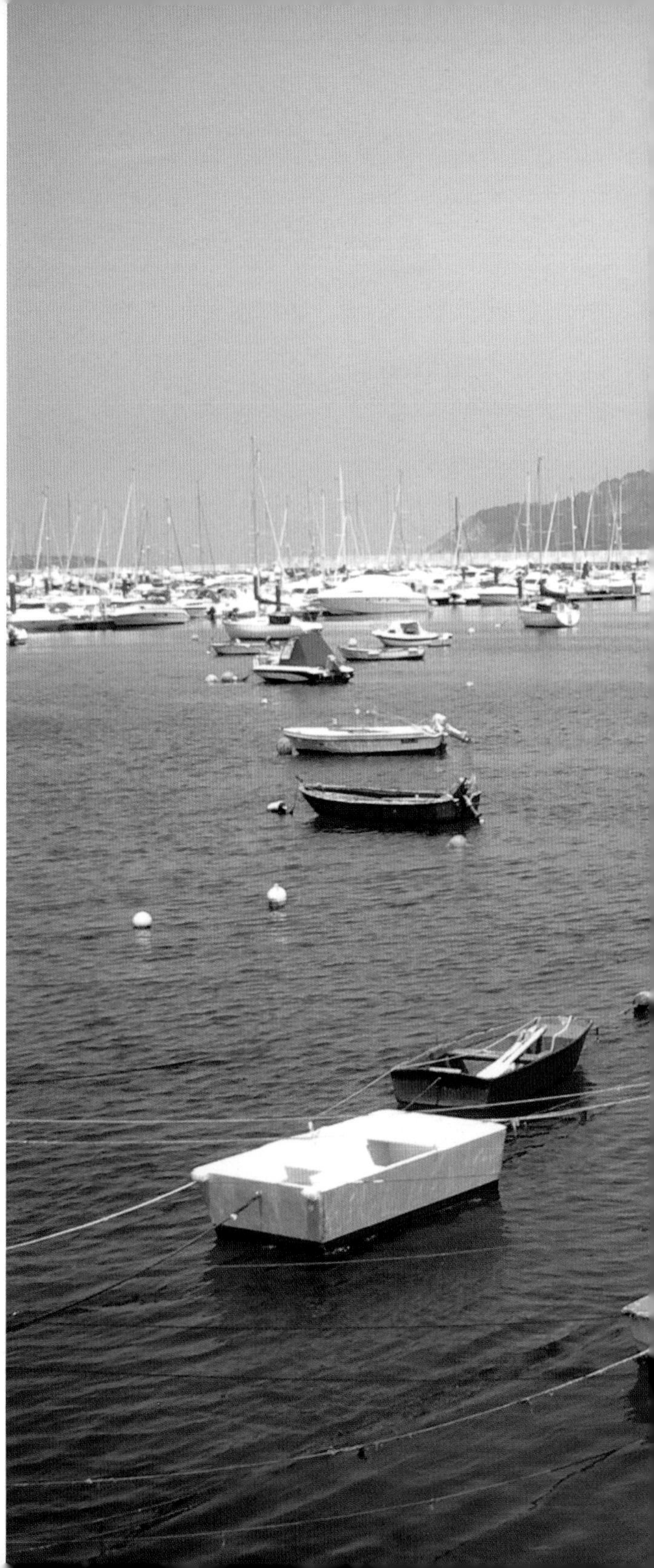

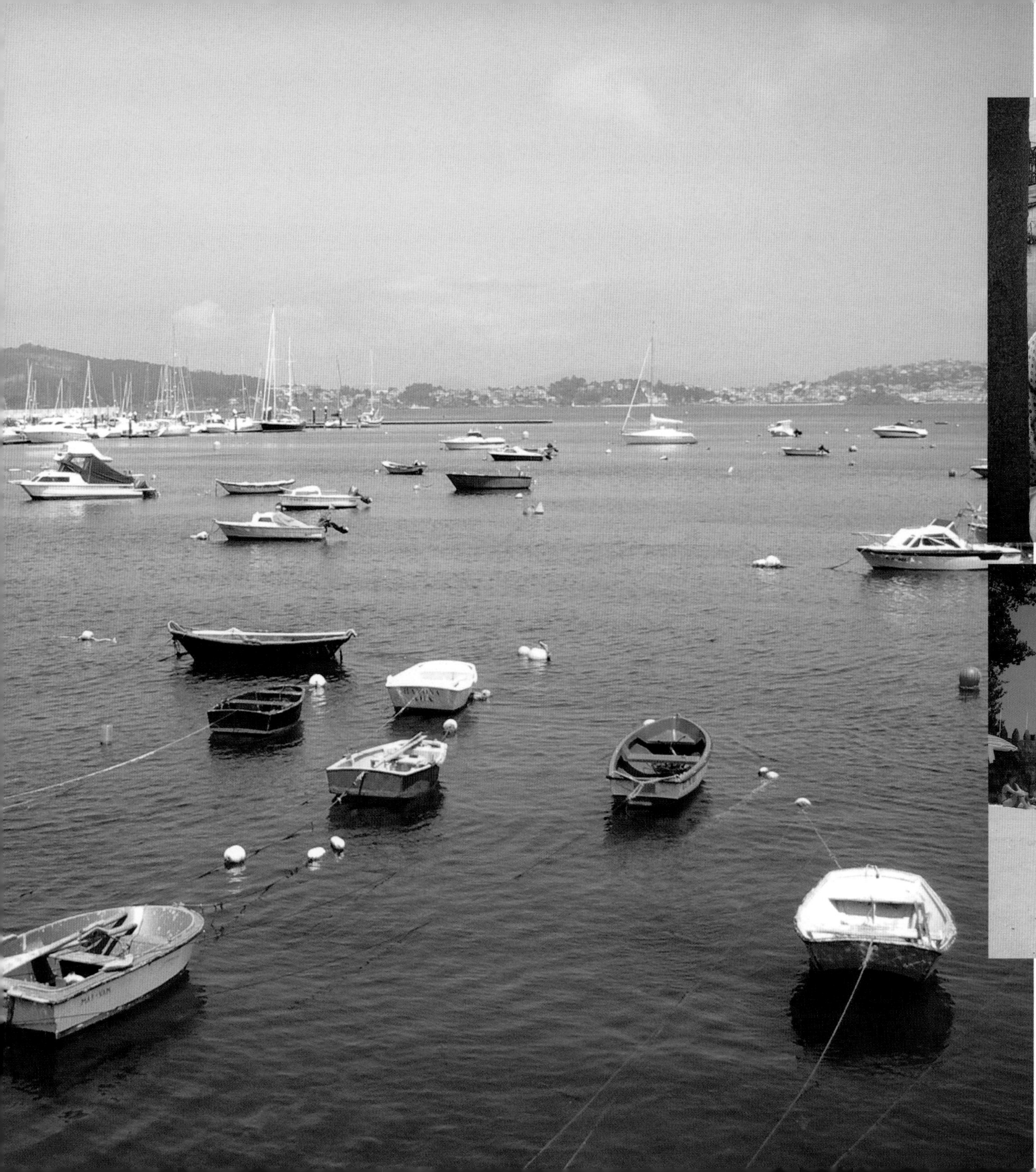

Left: Celtic Spirit *on the marina in Bayona, (blue hull with the tallest mast in the middle of the shot).* | ***Above:*** *(left) Ansis enjoying a coffee in a street-side café.* | *(right) One of the many tapas bars on the streets of Bayona.* | *(bottom) The beach next to Bayona Yacht Club.*

Spain to Portugal

The dramatic landscape of the shoreline of Galicia, northwest Spain, suddenly gives way to the rather featureless and flat landscape of the Portuguese coast.

14/07/06

At daybreak we enter the mouth of River Douro and make our way up to Porto. We tie up *Celtic Spirit* on the north quay wall just behind the 'Robelo' boats, which, in their day, were used to ferry port wine but nowadays ply their trade as tourist craft along the river. The riverside part of Porto, the Bairro district of Riberia is now a UNESCO World heritage site. This is an ancient part of the city where all the famous port producers are located on the south bank of the river while on the north quay you will find buildings that have stood there for hundreds of years and are still occupied by local residents. This is a beautiful and charming old city and an absolute must when sailing to Portugal. We discovered a new alcoholic beverage: white port and tonic, ice and lemon. This is a very popular drink here and for weeks to come it would replace our normal landfall tipple of gin and tonic. We watch children leaping from the iron bridge ahead of us (which we reckoned must be at least 50 m in height) and plunge feet first into the fast moving river Douro below. It was frightening just to watch. Ansis made a new friend, Victor, who introduced us to the best watering holes in the area and who partied with us and his friends on board *Celtic Spirit* on our last evening here.

Opposite page: *Bridge over Porto River from the top of our mast.*
Above and top right: Celtic Spirit *approaches the bridge. / The Douro River.*

17/07/06

We departed Porto on the tide yesterday evening a little the worse for wear and arrived at the mouth of the river Tega late in the afternoon today, having had a pleasant sail down the coast. Two hours later would see us berthed in Doca de Alcantara in the heart of Lisbon, not an easy task as the pontoons here are not numbered so it can be difficult to find one's allocated berth. Lisbon is an old and bustling city and it is very warm in mid-summer. Here *Celtic Spirit* would remain for three weeks while the skipper Michael would return to Ireland to help with the planning of our onward voyage to Antarctica. Janet was back in Dublin, was already very busy behind the scenes, co-ordinating the huge logistics of this massive undertaking, which would take up to another year to complete.

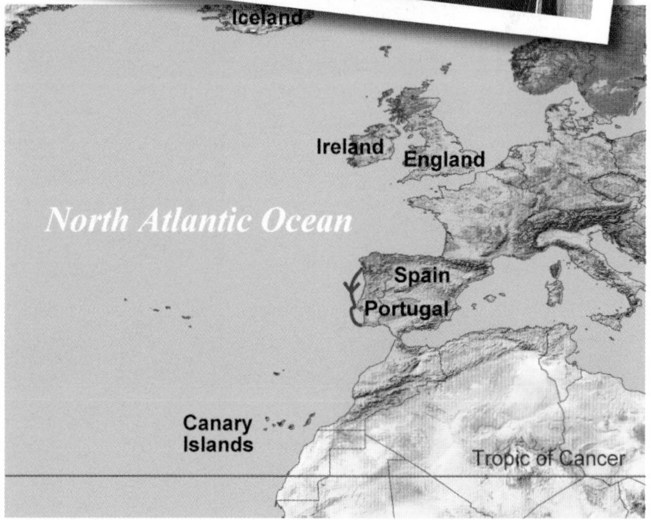

Clockwise from top left: *The ancient buildings of Porto. / The town of Porto stretches up the hill. / Robelo boats on the river. / Blayney sits on the aft deck of* Celtic Spirit *where she is tied alongside on the river in Porto,*

Clockwise from top left: *The lighthouse at Cape St Vincent.* / *Michiel's sketch of Lisbon.* / Celtic Spirit, *the biggest yacht at anchor outside the marina at Beleria.* / *Cape St Vincent through the heat haze.*

09/08/06

After departing Lisbon we made overnight stops in Sesimbru and Sines, we passed Cape St Vincent, the most southwesterly part of Europe and had brief stays in Beleria and Lagos before we arrived in Villamoura.

... this place makes a cemetery look and feel like a rock festival

Blayney on Sines

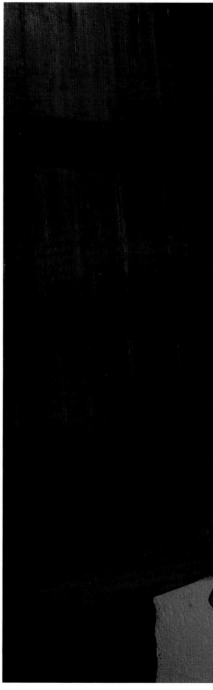

13/08/06

Villamoura was to be our last port of call in mainland Europe and the last opportunity to iron out all the remaining technical issues on the boat. For most of us, Villamoura was the beginning of the real voyage south to Antarctica. The skipper arranged for the boat to receive a maritime blessing by Father Tom Stack who had spent much time in southern Portugal as a young priest and who retains all his original connections.

Clockwise from top left: *Crew and friends. / Bottles and glasses of port laid out for tasting at Croft vineyard. / Taylor's, one of the oldest and most famous port houses.*

Clockwise from above:
Dusty bottles of vintage port.
| Barrels of port in the cellar.
| Ansis tests his strength and carries a barrel of port.

Portugal to Canary Islands

Leaving Villamoura, Portugal marks the start of a more serious drive southward in order to take advantage of weather conditions and arrive in Antarctica during the summer months of the southern hemisphere. Most crew will now stay on board for the rest of the trip as the length of sailing time increases.

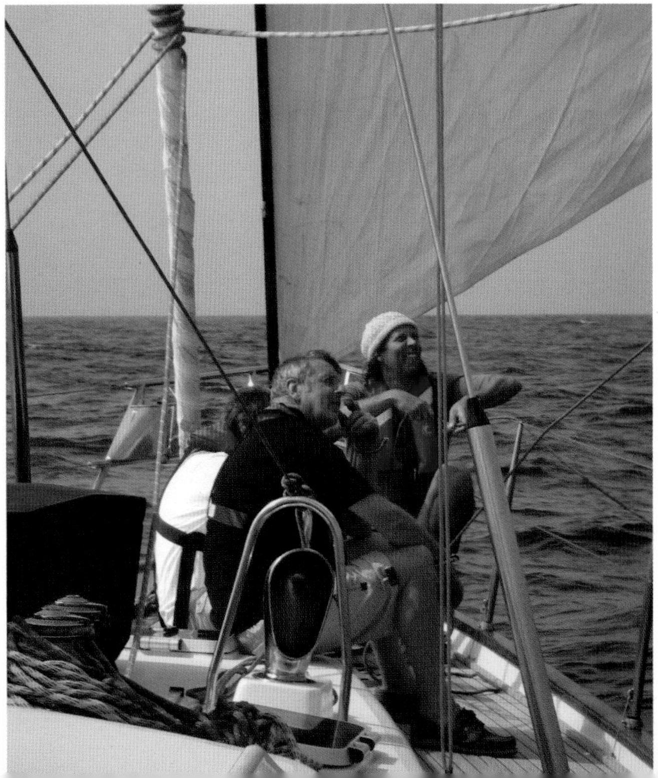

29/08/06

At 0400 this morning our alarm clocks sounded and our journey to the Canaries began with 1,500 miles to go. We cast off in the dark and headed out of the marina at 0500. The mizzen and main were raised as we headed into a very gentle breeze. Just as we thought we were near to waving Villamoura and mainland Europe goodbye the autopilot alarm went off, claiming we had rudder failure. There was a minor panic as we thought we had lost steerage completely and so we dropped anchor in 35 m of water in the darkness to investigate. We got out the emergency steering and attached this, having moved our dinghy out of the way. In the end, we realised that we had autopilot failure and thankfully not steerage failure which is far more serious. We decided to carry on sailing without a functioning autopilot. It may be a long sail yet to the Canaries without this useful extra 'person'. Tomorrow we will consult our manuals and attempt to resolve the issue. From midday we have a nice breeze of 15 knots from the northwest so we have gentle sailing of 7 knots with the main mizzen and two headsails flying. We encounter a lot of traffic heading out of the Mediterranean past Gibraltar on the way to the Atlantic Ocean. There were seven container ships in a row. Two of these caused us to

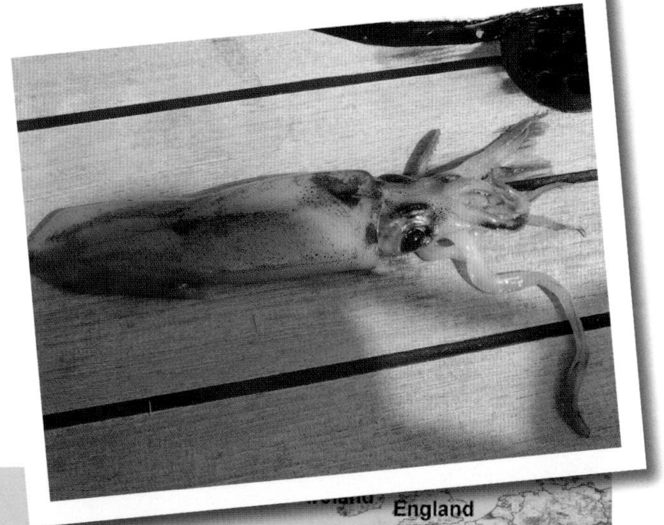

Opposite page: *Our mizzen spinnaker flies, adding colour to the ocean.* | ***Left and above:*** *Michael, Blayney and Michiel hold a foredeck committee meeting.* | *A small squid lands on deck.*

slow down (although *Celtic Spirit* had the right of way) allowing them to pass very close in front of us. Dinner of spaghetti bolognese ends a near perfect start to our main journey south to Antarctica.

30/08/06

Last night the new moon was with us for only a short while and the early hours of today were very dark. We are doing good speed, averaging over 7 knots with the winds coming up to 18 knots and over from abaft our stern. A reef was put in the main which makes helming easier. The sun came up around 0700. The nights are longer now. Today was a beautiful day with an awesome rolling sea of the most stunning blue. It is very warm especially down below. Finally we have our weather programme installed which is fantastic and it seems we have more of the same weather in store for the next few days. Hopefully we will get our spinnakers up tomorrow. We are now halfway to the Canaries and should arrive there on the weekend.

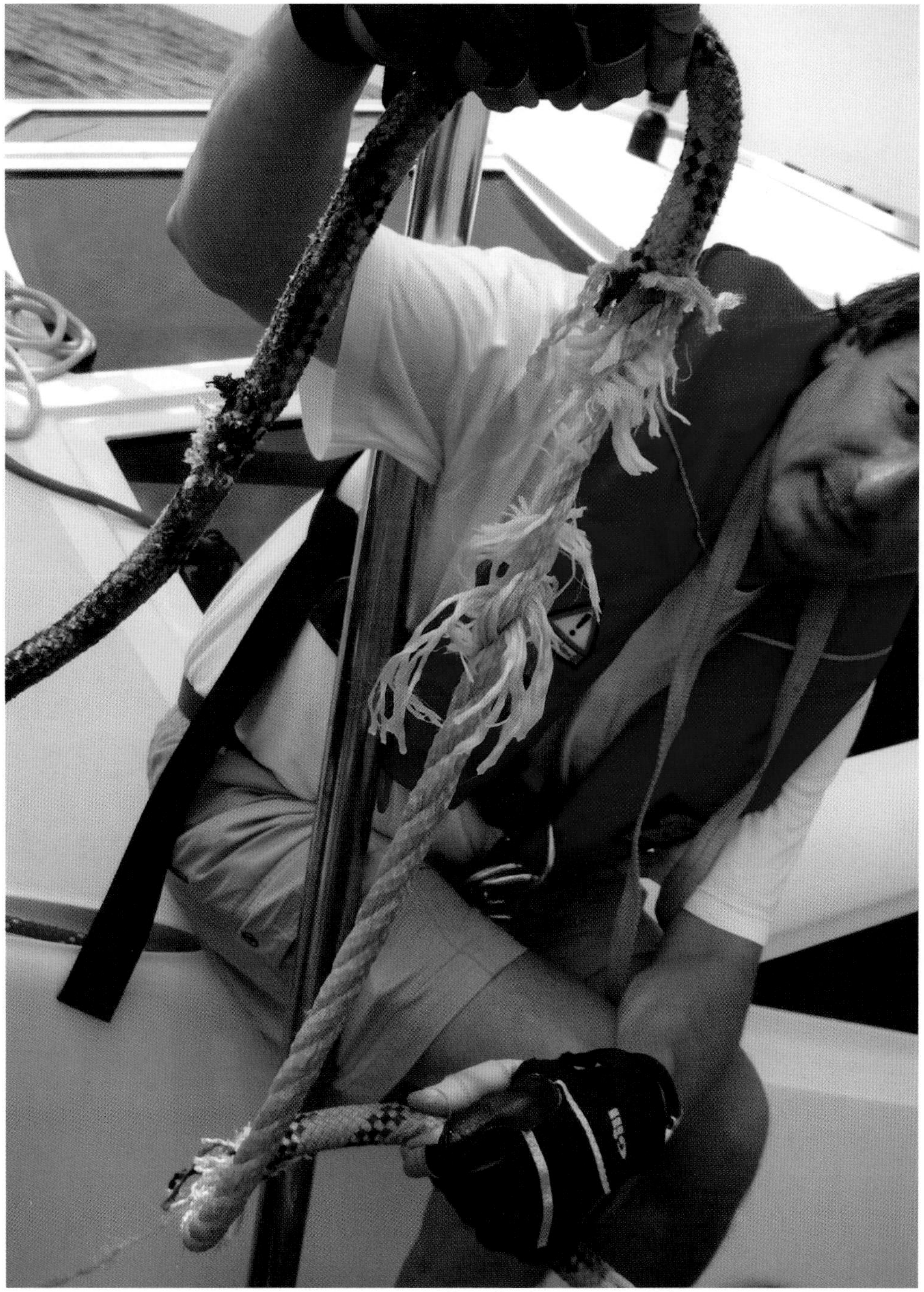

Opposite page: *(clockwise from bottom left) Preparations before Ansis dives below the boat. / Almost ready. / Ansis dives to free the sheet and prop. / Ansis feels the pull of a strong tide and swell as he tries to get back onboard.*

Left and above: *Michael inspects the damage done to our genoa sheet. / Ansis, Michiel and Tineke attempt to repair the damaged sheet.*

31/08/06

Today brought us light winds and we decided it was time to fly our two asymmetrical spinnakers, one from each mast. Working together with all hands on deck, we hoist the spinnakers. However, after some time, we decide to take them down as we are unable to maintain our desired course. We got the mizzen spinnaker down first, then the forward spinnaker, all with relatively little fuss. Just as we are packing away the forward spinnaker the radar bleeper falls from the mizzen mast and bounces off the deck into the water (the boat yard technicians did not refit it properly). Man Overboard drill is now in action! The engine is engaged and refuses to rev. We notice one of our genoa sheets is under the boat, caught around the prop! We have to sail to our man overboard under main and mizzen and staysail in light winds and a 2 m swell. Our 'man' is retrieved from the beam of the boat as we sail very slowly downwind by 'him'. All sails come down for the serious job of freeing the prop. Fortunately *Celtic Spirit* carries a diving compressor and in no time our fittest crew member was in a suit with weights, tethered and put into the water. With the strong swell and tide it is imperative that Ansis is tied on by line to the boat or he could easily be swept away. He also has a line trailing in the water, which he can hold on to. Ansis manages to free the sheet without cutting it. After all this we were underway again with some 400 miles to go to complete this leg of our onward voyage south with some lessons learned about loose lines on deck!

01/09/06

We are under engine for six hours for the first time in four days but our diesel is low and we have to go back to sailing even though the wind is astern and only 4 to 10 knots. This is also the fourth day without

Clockwise from above: *Michiel's patience pays off as he gets a bite on his line and reels in his fish. / Michiel is delighted with his catch. / Dorade for dinner. / Tuna for lunch tomorrow. / Gutting the catch of the day.*

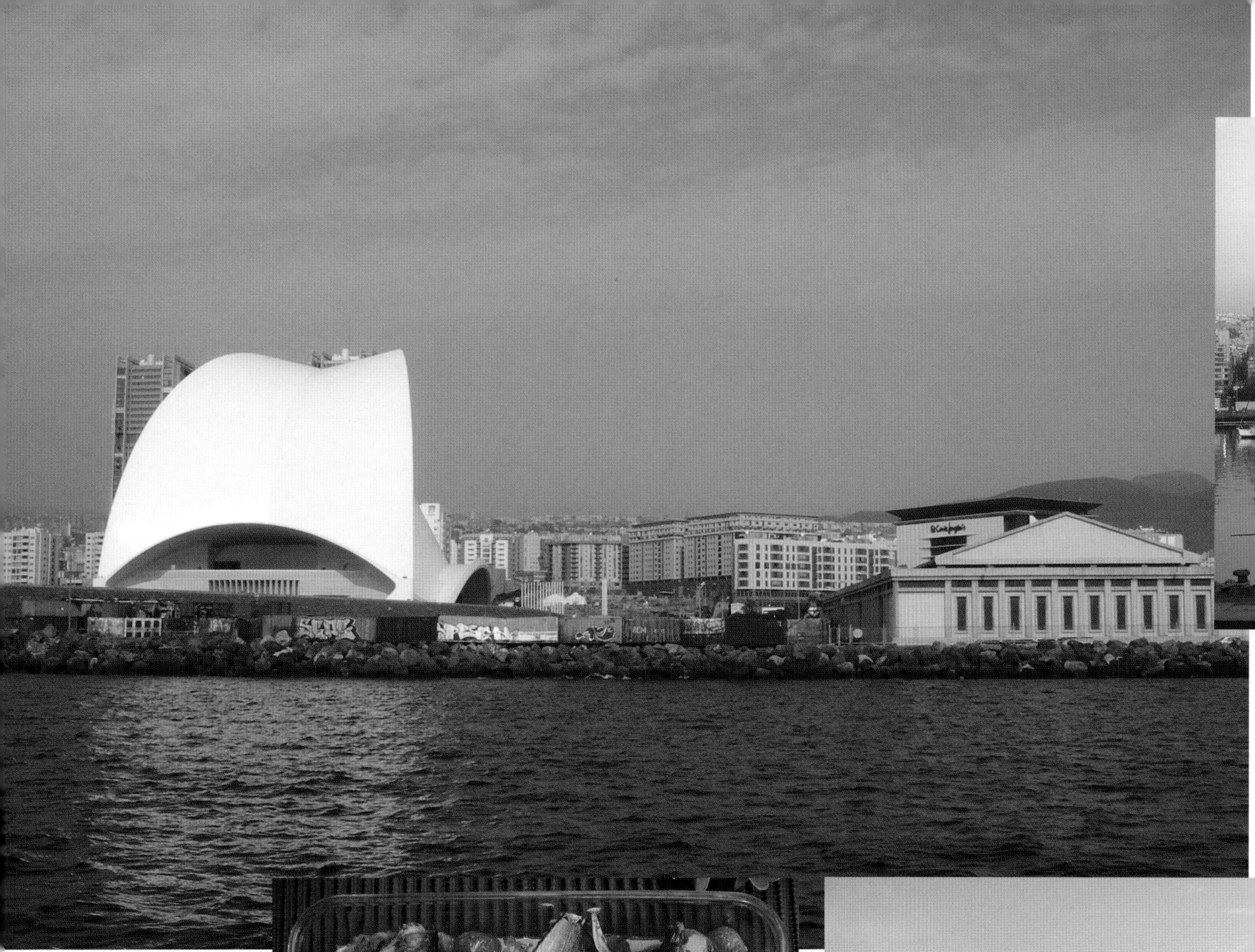

autopilot and we must hand steer twenty-four hours a day. Everyone is now used to spending up to six hours a day at the helm. Goosewinged and poled out, the genny gives us an average speed of 5 knots with 130 miles to go. The bonus of a slow speed is that our fishing has, for the first time, been successful – apart from the squid and flying fish voluntarily landing on our decks. The first fish caught was bright yellow in colour with a dark blue fin, possibly a dolphin fish, then we caught two good-sized tuna. We are looking forward to having them for lunch tomorrow. It has been a stunning day and more relaxed after yesterday's events.

Top: *(left and right) Arriving in Tenerife. /* Celtic Spirit *on the pontoon in the harbour (third boat from the right).*
Top: *(left and right) Fish for lunch / The entrance to Tenerife harbour.*

02/09/06

Today we arrived into Santa Cruz, Tenerife. While our skipper goes off with passports and checks in with the marina office, the crew set about cleaning the boat, heads, carpets and decks. It is very hot and humid and the town is surprisingly quiet. We have a delicious lunch of tuna and dolphin fish, expertly prepared by the catcher. This coming week will be spent preparing the boat for the next leg of our journey.

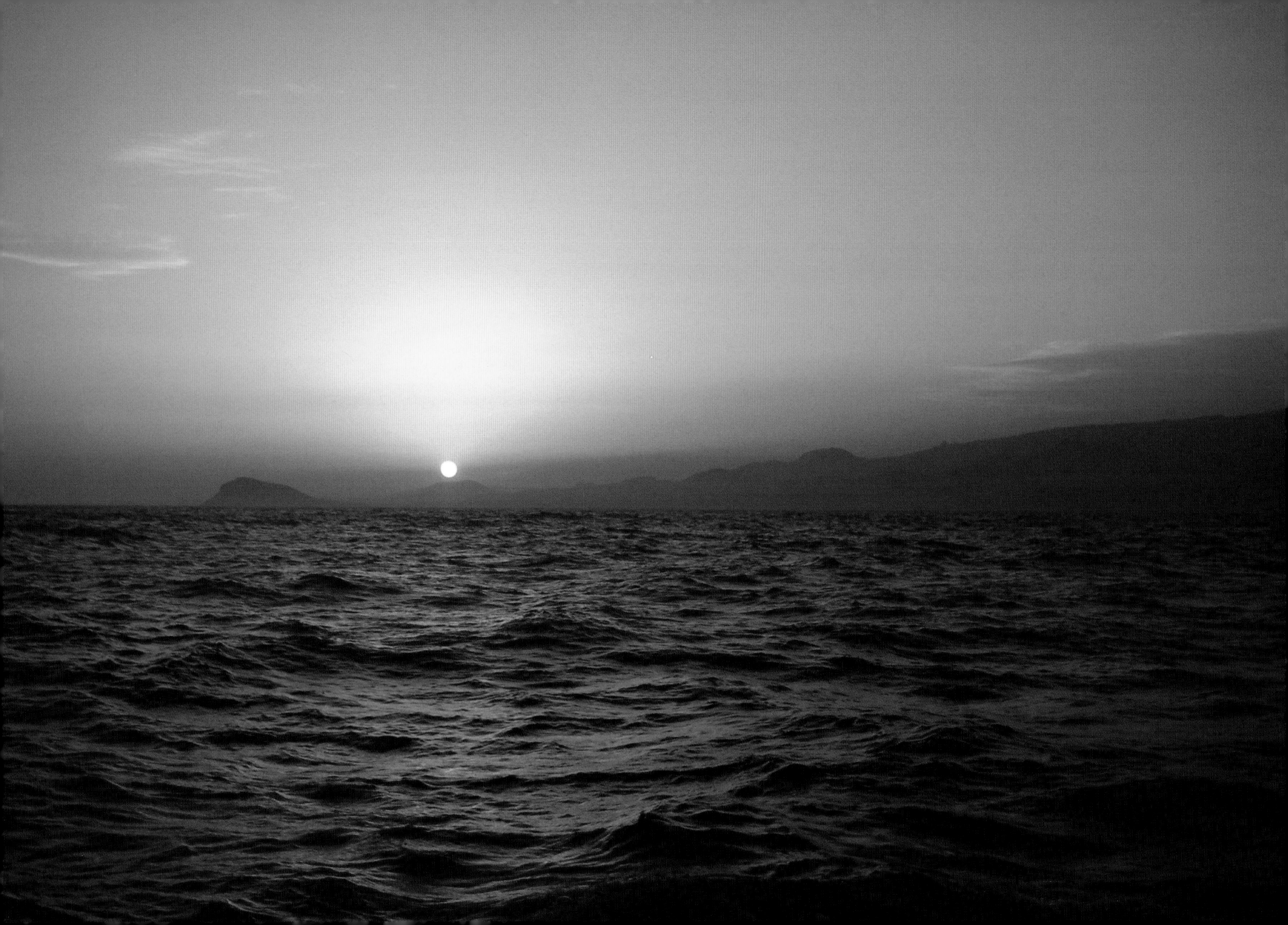

Canary Islands to the Cape Verde Islands

As we depart Tenerife, we leave behind civilisation as we know it. For the next few weeks, until we reach Salvador in Brazil, there will be no supermarkets or chandlers. From now on, we will have to be self sufficient and independent.

11/09/06

The week in Tenerife was spent preparing the boat for the next leg of the journey to the Cape Verdes, some 800 miles away. Trolley-loads of provisions were bought and stowed aboard the boat and we made sure to remove all cardboard and paper packaging, including labels, to avoid bringing cockroach eggs onboard. Fruit and vegetables were washed thoroughly. Despite our best efforts a cockroach was still spotting running around a cupboard. We now have 'roach hotels' in every conceivable place they may choose to lurk. Also taken on board was 3,500 litres of diesel and with full water tanks this brought the weight up by 8 tons.

We left Tenerife yesterday afternoon and by midnight we were saying goodbye to the last lights of the island. We had 25 knots as we departed but this was coming off the land and soon died, leaving us sloshing about for most of the night. The moon came up and was almost full so it made the night bright and pleasant.

It's a beautiful day today with blue skies and winds of between 10 and 16 knots from behind us. Main and mizzen are flying with the headsail goosewinged. We had dolphins playing on the bow wave for a short time this morning. The wind is slowly increasing and we are hoping for more to increase our boat speed. We covered just 150 miles on our first day, which is slow for *Celtic Spirit*.

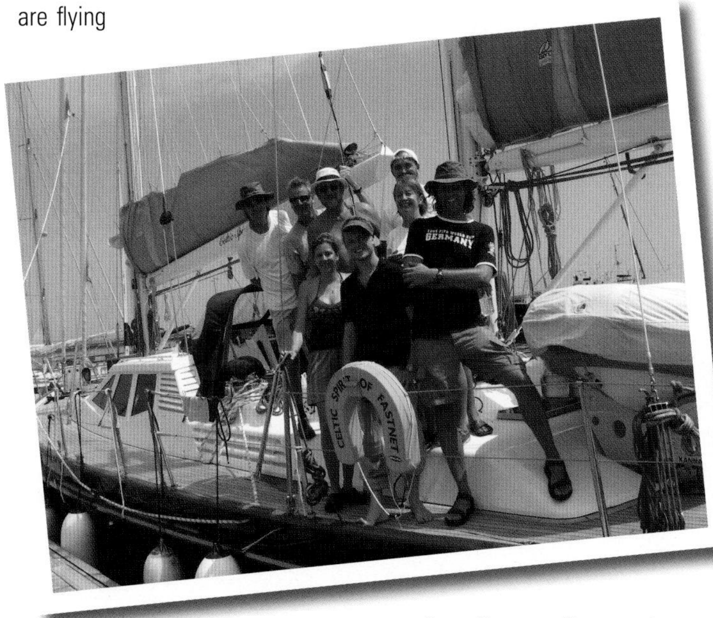

Opposite page: *The sun sets over Tenerife as we set sail for Cape Verde Islands.* | ***Above:*** *The crew just before we leave Tenerife, back row (left to right): Michael, Blayney, Denis and Ansis; front row (from left): Janet, JohnJohn, Vera and Michiel.*

12/09/06–14/09/06

We have had a very pleasant sail over the last few days and now it is only 150 miles to Palmeira on Ilha do Sal, Cape Verdes. Winds have been between 15 and 25 knots. However, on Wednesday night winds picked up to 35 knots forcing us to put reefs in all sails. The

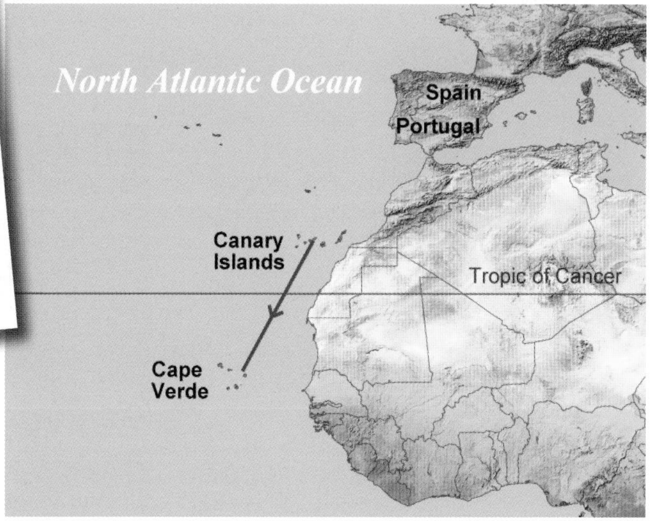

days have been mostly clear, sunny and hot. We have also had the moon out every night, which makes the night watches bright and enjoyable. Each night we have had more and more flying fish landing on board. During the day we can see them gliding over the water. They are replacing the squid that were throwing themselves on board a week ago. Although we are keeping a sharp lookout we have seen no whales as yet. However, we spotted a basking shark very close to the boat today. The two crew members who had their feet trailing in the water rapidly removed them!

We are being bombarded by flying fish. Two have struck crew in the cockpit while at least half a dozen others have thrown themselves on the decks.
Skipper's log entry

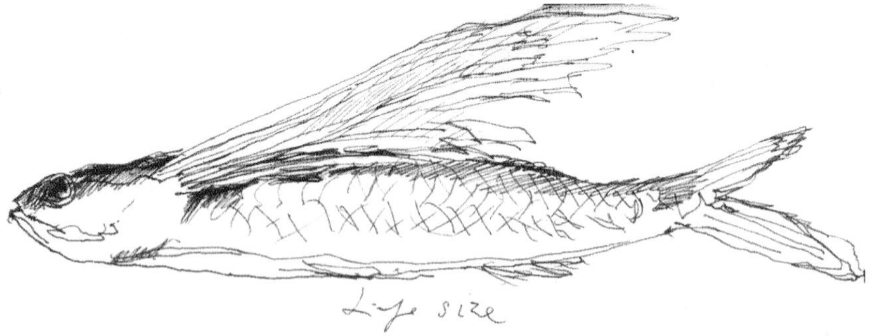

We are busy at this stage preparing for landfall, drawing up a list of repairs and maintenance chores including sewing up a small tear in our genoa. Our stay here will be brief before setting off for Salvador, Brazil.

Anticlockwise from top right: *Ansis showing the wingspan of a flying fish. / Flying fish where it has landed on deck. / On a plate with wings. / Flying fish de-winged and ready for frying...*

Left: *(top and bottom) The crew look on as we sail down the barren coast of Sal to Palmeira.* / *(above and middle) The volcanic peaks of Sal.*

Ashore was a sight to behold - a 'hamlet' with dirt tracks and the poorest of badly-constructed tiny dwellings. We had been led to believe by the pilot that we would have to go to the airport to clear in so we visited a

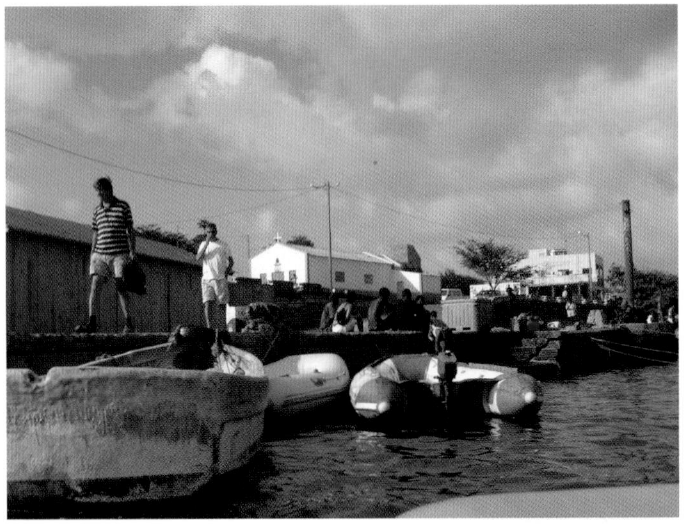

little shack of a shop to ask for a taxi. We were directed to the local police station where we had our papers stamped.

Skipper's log entry

Top: *(left) Michael and Blayney return to the dinghy after clearing in.* | *(right) The entry port of Palmeira and capital of Sal Island.*

Bottom: *(from left) Ansis goes to the rescue when we discover a large lump of rock sitting in our anchor.*

Clockwise from above: *Road to nowhere, leading out of Santa Maria. / The festival at night in full swing. / The view of the beach from our anchorage. / The stage for the music festival on the beach in Santa Maria.*

15/09/06–17/09/06

We arrive first into Palmeria, on Sal, Cape Verde in order to clear in and are lucky enough to find a local police official who stamps our passports. This saves us a taxi ride to the airport. This town is very small and poor and is really not much more than a shanty town. We are told that a festival is being hosted in Santa Maria on the south of the island, so we quickly weigh anchor and sail south in the late evening sun. On lifting the anchor we discover it has collected a large lump of coral. It takes a few attempts to rid the anchor of its cargo before we can be on our way. The landscape as we sail by is flat with several volcanic peaks. It looks rocky and barren with no trees. But it is not long before we arrive into Santa Maria and we drop our anchor as

MERCADO MUNICIPA

Opposite page: *(clockwise from bottom left) The streets of Santa Maria away from the palm tree perfect tourist resorts. / The municipal market where you can buy jewellery, art and fish.*

Clockwise from above: *Local children on the beach in Santa Maria. / Fishing boats. / A young boy with a dead eel fish. / A game of beach football.*

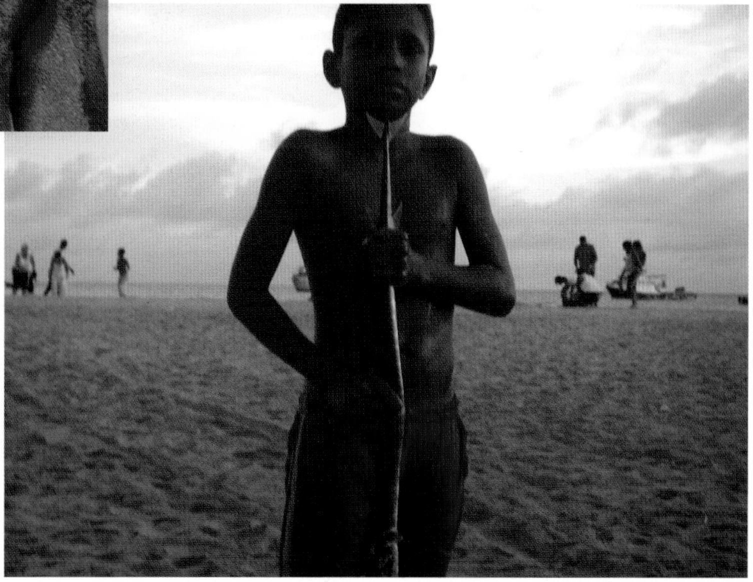

The anchor is raised from the sandy seabed, which at 10 m is clearly visible from the deck. There is only around 5 knots of wind and we have to take course 140 degrees to avoid the next island. Can't believe we're off to cross the Atlantic. Today the cast-off preparations are less painful than the previous ones in Lymington, Villamoura and Santa Cruz. No boxes on deck, just a massive wash down with the fire-fighting hose to get rid of all the sand from the beach landings in the dinghy, most of which were wet affairs because of the surf. One last-minute dash to shore to send those wet bent postcards and buy the CD that I heard in the café last night. Last café con leche and a swim in that 27 °C turquoise sea and off we go, all sails up.

Michiel's diary entry

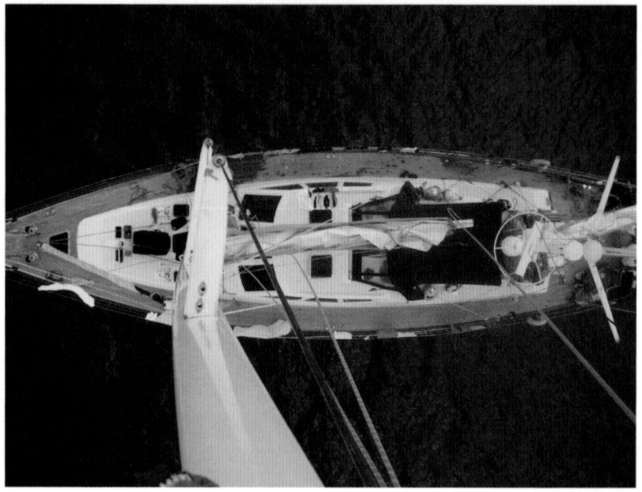

Top: The view of Santa Maria and Sal from the top of the mast.
Bottom: (from left) Michiel repairs the damaged sails. / The view of Celtic Spirit from the top of the mast.

darkness falls. The festival has begun. Music reaches us from the shore and we can see the stage and people on the beaches. We head for shore and find there is no pier or slip to tie up alongside or elegantly disembark so we have to ride the waves to land on the beach then pull the dinghy up to dry ground. This, of course, involves getting wet. Some enterprising locals offer to mind the dinghy for us for a small fee. We give them half the money and promise the other half later. When we do finally return we discover our good torch had been stolen. However, the local people are friendly and helpful and there was no trouble or even the usual festival drunkenness. The music and bands continue well into the next day without us as we retire to the boat, tired and in need of our sleep.

The mobile coverage here is restricted to a local network and most of our phones don't work. There are plenty of internet cafés and they have phones also but this is not cheap. Euros are accepted in most places (prices are quoted in Euro) as this has become a popular tourist destination with many Italians. There are a few new resort hotels along the beach. Power cuts are common as the supply cannot meet the demand. Our repairs and maintenance jobs are nearly complete and it will not be long now before we leave and are heading across the Atlantic and further south.

Above, right and far right:
Mlichiel takes his last swim, Celtic Spirit *at anchor and her tender making its way to shore.* / *Raphael our rasta friend and helper.* / Celtic Spirit *dinghy ashore.*

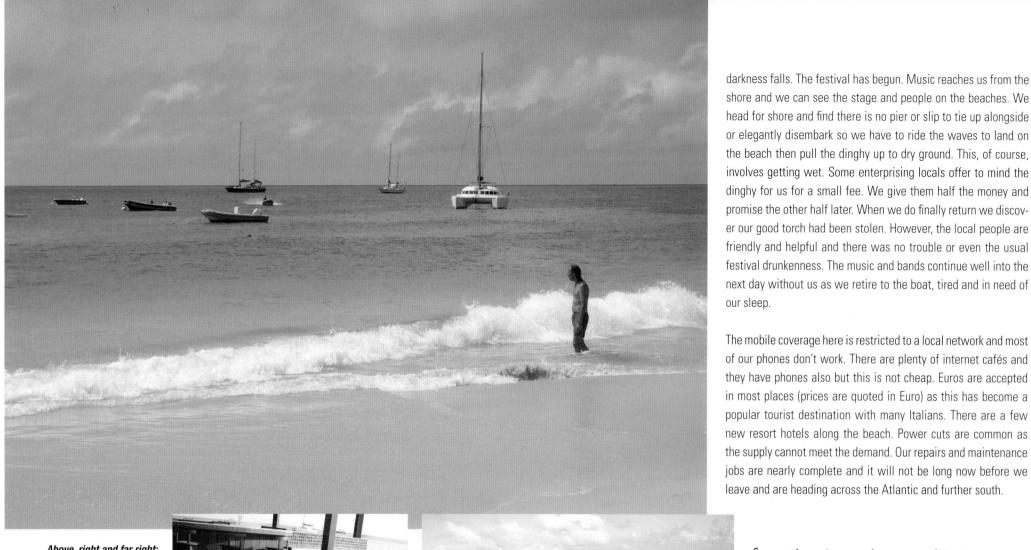

A most poignant moment for me was off the Cape Verde Islands. My grandfather from Lower Cove, Kinsale, Ireland, who was in the Merchant Navy, was buried at sea and being the first member of our family to revisit that spot, I cast a rose into the deep to commemorate him.

Vera's diary entry

Cape Verde Islands to Brazil

Our sail from the Cape Verde Islands to Brazil takes us across the Atlantic Ocean and the Equator. From the northern hemisphere to the southern hemisphere and to the continent of South America, this is our longest time at sea so far.

19/09/06–22/09/06

With all our maintenance and repairs done and Santa Maria's festival over, it was time to move on. We weighed anchor and headed south down past Boavista, which is a much larger island than Sal but with a smaller population. Everyone sat out on deck mesmerised by the passing scenery. With a shift in wind direction we gybed and headed west across the top of the other islands, Maio, Santiago, Fogo then gybed back down south between Fogo and Nova Sintra. This was our last sight of land. We brought out new charts to plot our Atlantic crossing and with mostly light winds we took the fishing rod out, ever hopeful we might catch something. The sea teemed with fish and we see them swimming next to the boat but the closest we have come to catching anything is having the bait completely bitten off the line. For a brief moment we also spotted a large turtle in the water. He stuck his head up out of the water but we had passed him by before we could photograph him.

Opposite page: *The coast of Boavista is our last sight of land before Brazil.*
Left and top right: *Janet and Tineke have a chat on deck. / Our plotter at the wheel shows our position and track as we make our way between the Islands.*

'A small piece of Sahara drifting in the Atlantic Ocean ...' It looks incredible from the sea, no habitation or roads visible, just white beaches and rugged hills of rock, less volcanic looking than Sal.

Michiel's diary entry

Everyone is settled into their routine and life as usual revolves around watches, food and weather. Being on watch means keeping a constant eye on wind speed and angle, and ensuring that we keep the boat speed up. The weather has continued to be hot (around 32 °C) and humid (around 75 per cent) but yesterday we were treated to a

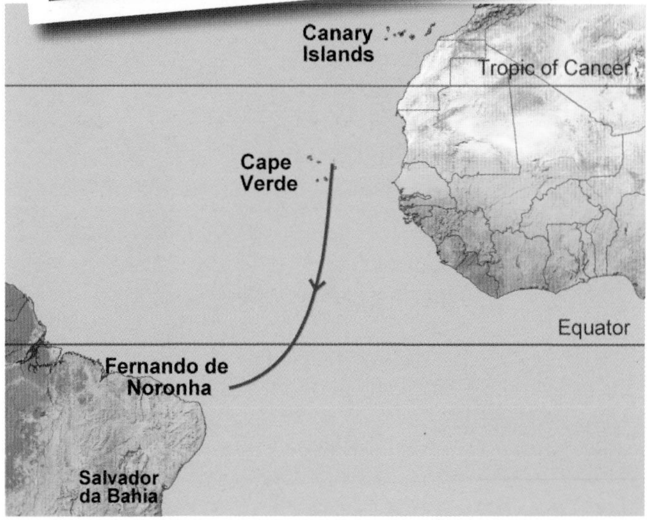

Spectacular sunrise with little wind and lots of cirrus and anvil clouds warning of weather to come. Batten down the hatches!

Michiel's diary entry

Top: *A squall on the horizon.* | ***Bottom:*** *(from left) The squall heads our way.* | *The horizon disappears in the rain.* | *Water pours off the boom.*

Clockwise from top left: *Blayney laughs in the rain while Ansis takes the helm. / JohnJohn, Michiel and Tineke cool down. / Blayney, Michiel and Tineke enjoy a cup of tea after the rain shower. / A hot cuppa and biscuits to dunk. / Michiel uses rain water caught in the mainsail for a fresh-water shower.*

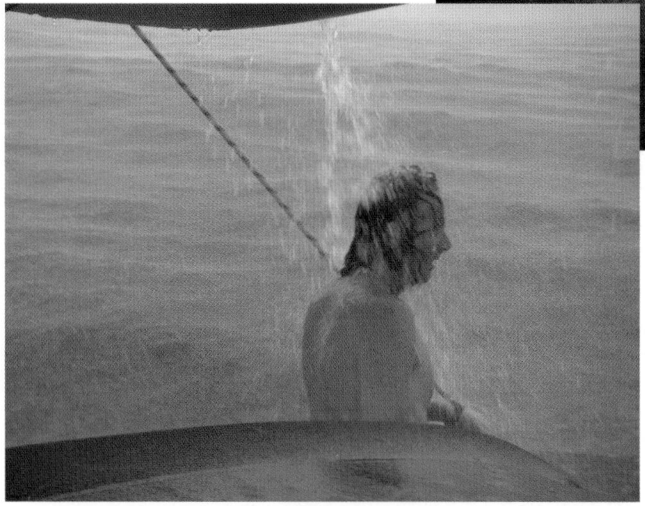

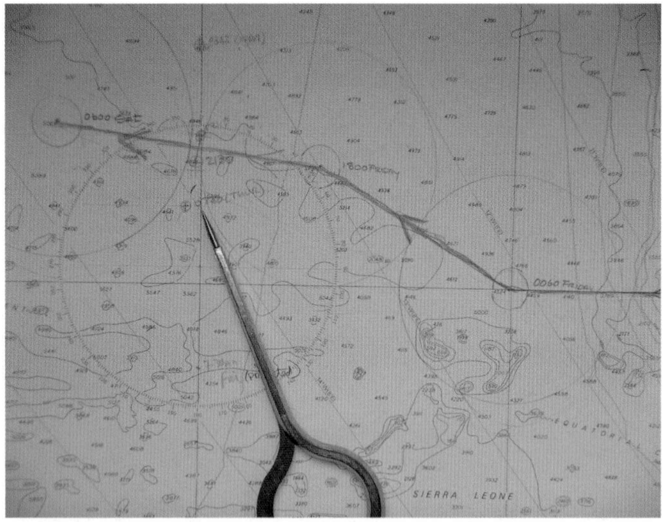

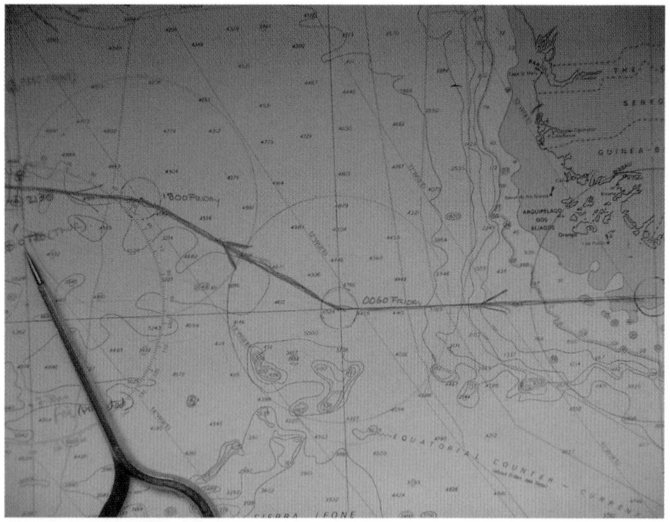

Clockwise from top left: *Laundry hangs out to dry. / The track of the forecast cyclone. / Grib files (downloadable weather forecast files) showing our forecast, the red feathers indicate very high winds (60 knots).*

rain shower. For some time in the distance we saw a dark cloud we thought would pass by but a sudden wind shift changed its course and this brought it straight into our path. The breeze picked up quickly and the rain came down harder and harder. Everyone got drenched and some of the crew decided to use this as their shower for the week! The wind dropped and shifted as quickly as it had risen and simultaneously the rain stopped. The front passed through in about thirty minutes and the wind did not increase much over 28 knots. It was the most exciting thing to happen since we had left the Cape Verde Islands and was a very welcome break from the heat we have been experiencing. We hit a few more squalls throughout the night but by the morning we were back to little wind and plenty of heat.

Left: *Time to get the storm sail ready for action.*
Below: *(from left) Ansis, Blayney, JohnJohn and Michiel attach the storm sail. / Weather comes in and our sail is attached and set to go in the pink bag at the mast.*

Our weather forecast has shown a tropical storm of Force 11 building up off the coast of Guinea, Africa and it is projected to come our way by Friday. It is 300 miles in diameter. We prepare our storm sail and set it up by the mast. In the meantime, the skipper reroutes our course directly south in the hope that the storm will pass to the north of us. We make as much speed as possible over the next forty-eight hours and thankfully our tactic pays off.

We are now heading into the doldrums although with the very light winds we have been experiencing we feel we are already there! Our colourful blue and yellow spinnaker looks fantastic in the middle of the ocean.

23/09/06–27/09/06

Finally our doldrums have given way and we now have the trade winds from the southeast. After a few days of evening squalls and overcast days the sun has made a welcome appearance.

We crossed a major shipping route mid-Atlantic and for a few days encountered container ships, some of which came quite close at times, forcing us to make contact to find out their intended path. These ships are huge and move at a rapid pace.

We had a more serious issue one day when we realised that the fridge freezer system was not working. There was much peering into dark holes and manuals and speculation as to the cause, including a theory that the gas had gone. Plans were put in place to eat the food that will go off the quickest but following emergency emails to the manufacturers it was discovered that an airlock created in heavy seas was the problem. Our food supplies

Clockwise from right: *King Neptune's cardboard trident. / Michael our skipper dressed up as King Neptune. / The pot of 'hoosh' for our ceremony. / The vast blue waters of the Equator. / Our GPS reading at the Equator.*

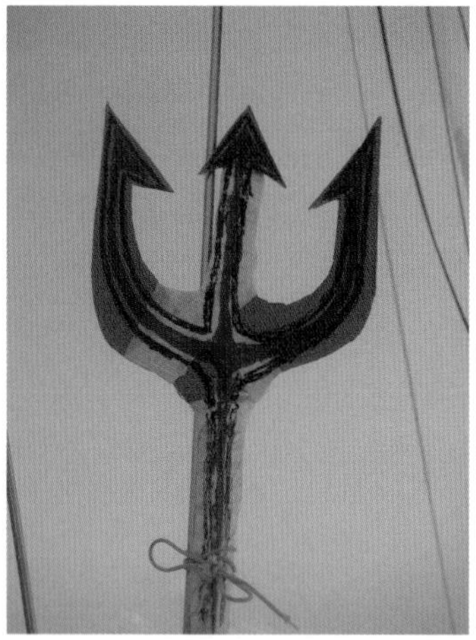

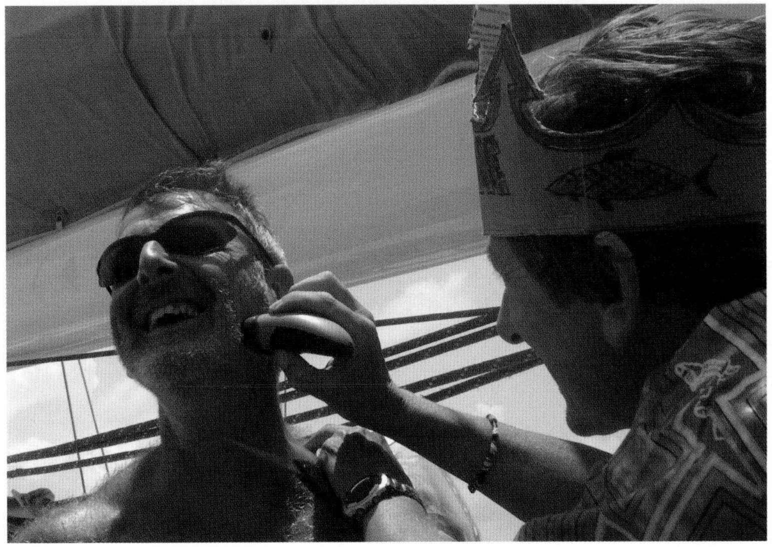
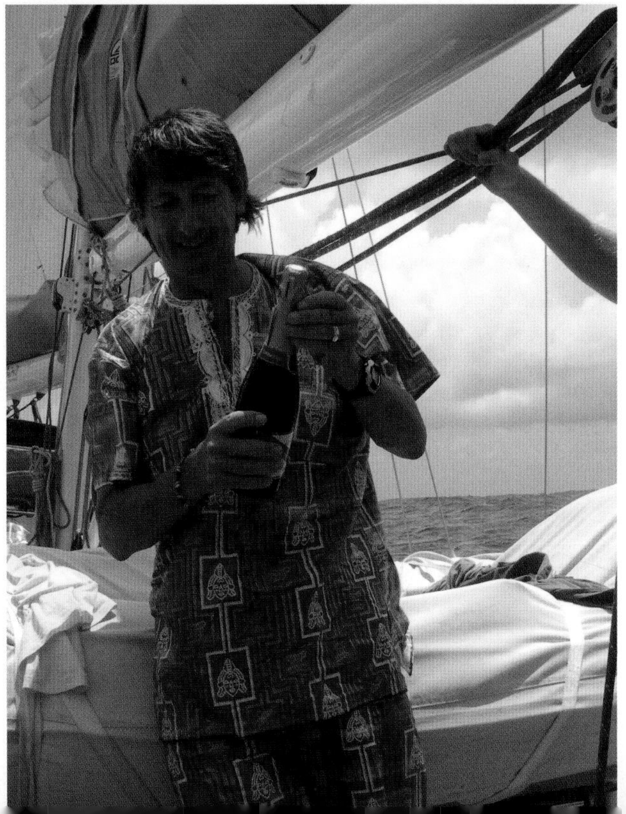

Clockwise from top left: *Tineke and JohnJohn have a spoonful of 'hoosh'. / Michiel and Ansis have locks of their hair cut off. / The skipper opens a bottle of champagne. / Blayney has a part of his beard shaved off.*

are diminishing slowly but although there is no fruit left, there is still plenty of food to be had onboard so we will definitely not starve.

We passed Peter and Paul rocks (1° N 30° W) in the early hours of Monday morning and yesterday at 1231 UT we crossed the Equator, that imaginary line separating the northern and southern hemispheres. Preparations have been in hand and with our skipper dressed as King Neptune, complete with African suit, cardboard crown and trident made from cardboard lashed to the boat hook, the initiation rites commence on the aft deck. According to tradition the equatorial virgins – those who have yet to cross the equator – or slimy Pollywogs as they are known must pass this initiation ritual before being deemed a Shellback. Our King Neptune goes through the crew individually, proclaiming each one's crimes and then dishes out our punishments. He cuts off locks of hair, part-shaves beards and forces us to drink spoonfuls of disgusting 'hoosh', a concoction of bitter lemon juice, beans and corn, all which went into the pot and to which he added the locks of hair! When he is done we 'mutiny' and surprisingly, King Neptune actually feels quite unwell after drinking the hoosh! Certificates

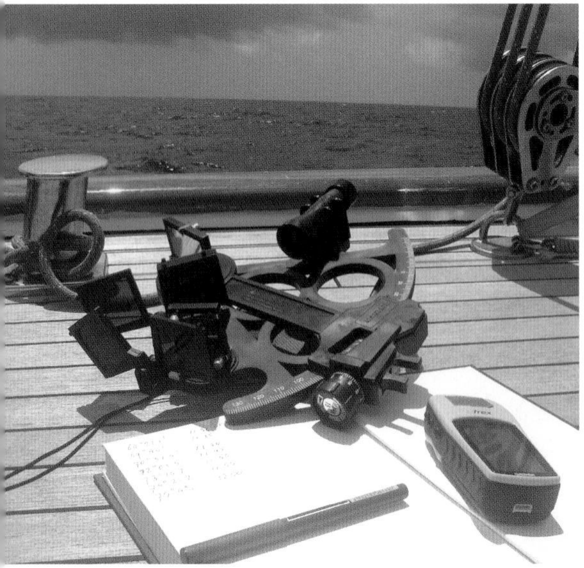

Clockwise from top left: *Blayney writes an email home. / Michiel sketches while Tineke relaxes with a book. / JohnJohn goes for a mid-Atlantic swim. / New and old, modern-day hand held GPS and the way it was done in years gone by – a sextant.*

Right: *(top) The spinnaker catches water as we blast along the ocean. / (bottom) Sunset in the Atlantic.*
Below: *(top) A bird follows us for a while. / (bottom) Michiel takes a sun sight as he practises his celestial navigation.*

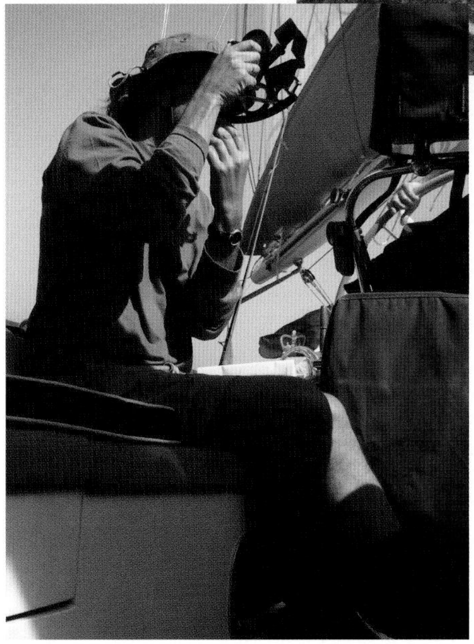

are given out to confirm the crossing as a bottle of champagne is opened and shared among the crew.

We are now en route to an island off the coast of Brazil called Fernando de Noronha (3°50′ S 32°24′ W). It is reported to be one of the most beautiful places on earth, full of dolphins, turtles and is a top spot for scuba diving. The crew are very much looking forward to this landfall. Formalities might prove to be an issue, as it is not recognised as an official port of entry to Brazil. Arriving on the South American continent represents more than 7,100 miles sailed since Arctic Iceland.

Fernando de Noronha

After nine days at sea we arrive at the tropical paradise and national marine park of Fernando de Noronha, off the north-east coast of Brazil, our first landfall in the southern hemisphere. Volcanic mountain peaks reach out of the ocean, rich in history and marine wildlife.

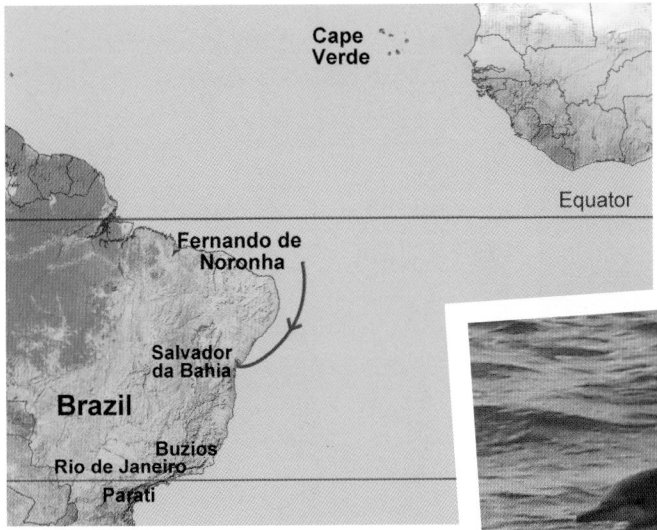

28/09/06–02/10/06

In the early hours of the morning the island of Fernando de Noronha came into view. The sun was not yet up, making it difficult to find our way to an anchorage, although we could see the shape of the island with its unusual dramatic peaks. This island is one of the few places on the planet that is a UNESCO World Heritage Site and visitor numbers are severely restricted.

As dawn broke we could see many yachts at anchor. We learned this was the annual racing regatta of yachts from mainland Brazil. Swimming in and around the boats were scores of spinner dolphins unique to this island. We dropped anchor in St Anthony's Bay and launched the dinghy. Two crew members were dispatched to find out about formalities. They spoke to a couple of neighbouring boats, both of whom advised us to avoid the officials as this was not an official port of entry to Brazil. We should have cleared into one of the major ports in Brazil hundreds of miles away before arriving here. On this advice we decided to keep a low profile. A dinghy ride took us over to the little harbour, sheepishly past the sentry box of officialdom and then it was a short walk up the hill lined with open air bars and stalls selling everything a visitor might want. We took a 'cab' ride (in the form of a beach buggy) to find

Opposite page: *Conceição Beach overlooked by Mount Pico.* | **Right and top right:** *Spinner dolphin in St Anthony's Bay.* | *Fernando de Noronha as dawn breaks.*

My favourite place:
Fernando de Noronha – awesome beaches, people, wildlife and atmosphere (and beach buggies), such a cool remote island, I am definitely going back there some day. Hopefully that Brazilian guy who taught me how to dance and nearly bit my ear off isn't still there then!

Tineke Berthelsen

Clockwise from above: *Michiel's illustration of a boat at anchor in St Anthoy's Bay. / The view out into the ocean. / Our modes of transport – hire car and cab. / JohnJohn, Michael and Blayney outside the church in the town centre. / A herd of cows making their way through the town centre. / Sculpture garden with monsters from the deep.*

Anticlockwise from top left: *Baia do Sueste which has a large turtle population. / Underwater shots of fish in Baia do Sueste. / Beach side bar and restaurant. / Michiel drinks from a coconut.*

the main part of 'town' and were dropped off at the Banco Real, the only bank on the island. We were baffled as to the purpose of this little bank as it does not exchange money nor does its ATM accept any foreign cards! Eventually, we exchanged our money for local currency at the island's small airport.

While visiting this island we went to a beach known for its turtle population to go snorkelling and swimming in the sheltered bay. On a visit to another beach some members of the crew hired surfboards and a body board and tried their hands at riding the waves. Despite their lack of experience they persevered but found themselves beaten and semi-drowned by the big swell and breaking waves and after several dunkings called it a day. We came across several beach huts where we watched the sun going down while enjoying a beer and admiring the island's beautiful and dramatic landscape. The perfect end to a day. We ate dinner in a *pousada* (small accommodation units characterised by the hammocks hanging everywhere) on our last evening and after our meal, the waitress told us there would be music in the square until the small hours. The music was forró (also the name of a dance style), which has a kind of Brazilian/Cajun sound but to most of us it all sounded like the same song played without a break. The music is obviously popular as all the locals were dancing to it.

This island with its beautiful beaches and palm trees, turtles and spinner dolphins, although basic, is charming and on closer inspection it draws you in to its hidden treasures. As a National Sea Park it has avoided development, which would spoil its rustic atmosphere. We were sad to say goodbye.

I am glad I am not a prisoner or an enemy ship in this bay as neither would stand a chance. Frigate birds fly overhead and dolphins swim by in the turquoise sea below, some jumping out like spinning tops.
A long-tailed bird hovers around the cliff and a small mammal creeps around the cannons.
Michiel's diary entry

Clockwise from top left: *Cove rock formation. | Waves breaking on the Conceição Beach. | Beach Bar tucked under palm trees and tropical jungle. | Drawing of the cannon at the ruins of the fort on the hill top overlooking the bay. | Detail of the cannon.*

Clockwise from bottom left: *Lifeguards keep a watch out on the best surfing beach on the island. / The boys try their hand at surfing. / Beautiful unspoiled beaches. / The boys return the dinghy to the sea. / St Anthony's Bay and our anchorage.*

Salvador da Bahia

From Fernando de Noronha we sailed to Salvador on the north-east coast of Brazil where* Celtic Spirit *stayed for two weeks while the crew explored the city and surrounds. After this, we sailed further south stopping briefly in the idyllic Buzios before heading on to Rio.

01/10/06–05/10/06

As darkness fell *Celtic Spirit* set off from Fernando de Noronha for Salvador into 25 knots of wind from the southeast. We were beating on a port tack in the established trade winds for the next three days and then changed course for Salvador which saw us on a down wind run for the following two days until we reached our destination. During our first three days we made excellent progress sailing mostly at 9 knots. The weather was good and with the benefit of a full moon night watches were a pleasure.

Around 0600 on the morning of 5 October we rounded the headland into Baia de Todos os Santos and headed towards Salvador. We dropped anchor and launched the dingy so that the skipper and first mate could get the lie of the land ashore. They returned after visiting the harbour master's office and organising our berth as well as checking the depths as we were now at low water and *Celtic Spirit's* draft would just about clear the bottom.

Opposite page and above:
The skyline of Salvador. / Celtic Spirit *arrives into the marina in Salvador.*

I can see the lights of Brazil. We are ghosting along at 5 knots; wind 12-15 knots from the east. It has been almost a run for the last two days. Before that, a broad reach with 20 knots wind charged us along. The first two days from Fernando moving south were a beat so we were living on a fast-moving slope. It is hot during the day (up to 35 °C) but humidity is lower now.

At 0500 we round into the Bay of Salvador and see the light come up over the skyscrapers. It is low tide and down goes the anchor outside Bahia Marina pier. Exploring by dinghy the skipper decides to go into Marinho du Brazil, which looks more fun being just outside the lift to the upper town. All crew have to go to the police, then customs, then health, then Navy Port Captain who all use a lot of paper, photocopying, carbon paper, stamps and staples.

Michiel's diary entry

The Brazilian authorities demand that visitors clear in with four different authorities: Immigration, Customs, Health and Port Captain in this order. All crewmembers were required to attend the Policia Federal for immigration where we had to sit and wait while all our details were recorded on computer and paper and our visas issued. When we got to the Customs offices they are closed until after lunch so we had to wait until then. At the health department offices it took some persuading for us not to be given injections as the doctor was convinced that we required Yellow Fever vaccines because we had come from the Cape Verde Islands. This was untrue and having consulted his books we were granted that all important piece of paper with the official stamp of clearance. Then it was back to the harbour master's office (Capitania dos Portos) to prove that we had visited all the authorities and had the necessary paperwork. This process of visiting all these offices took a full day!

Salvador was the capital of Brazil until 1763. At one time it was the second most important city in the Portuguese Empire. It was a major slave-trading centre and today this is reflected in its African culture. This is black Brazil and its influence can be seen in the music, the

Above and right from top to bottom: *Marina Nautica da Bahia. / Dealing with officialdom: immigration, customs and health.*

Left, below and bottom right: *The lift that brings you to the Pelourinho District. / Cold beer! / View from the marina up to 'the old town of Pelourinho'.*

Salvador BAHIA

Top: *(from left) Salvador's old town – the Pelourinho District. / Street vendors.*
Bottom: *(from left) The streets around the marina. / Couples dancing in the market to a street band.*

Above: *(top, centre and bottom) JohnJohn and Tineke walking the streets in Itaparica. / Walking down the pier to the ferry in tropical rain. / Tineke on the ferry trip back to Salvador.*
Right: *(top) The busy beach in Itaparica. / (bottom) Fishmongers doing business.*

Above: *The view from the top of the lift down over the marina area and bay.* | ***Bottom:*** *Schooners on the marina – these boats arrive early in the morning, take tourists on trips for the day and arrive back in the evening.* | ***Top right:*** *Michael, Blayney and JohnJohn at the fuel depot filling* Celtic Spirit's *tanks before leaving Salvador.*

food, and the culture. The old city, the Pelourinho District, where we spent much of our time, is very run down and is similar to Havana, Cuba. Many of the street people have gone and the fevelas (shanty settlements) have been removed around the harbour area. There is a strong police presence on the streets to protect tourists but caution is still very much required. A taxi-driver told us that between 10 p.m. and 7 a.m. cars can drive through red lights because it is more dangerous to stop at night than to disobey the rules of the road! However, we don't let all this caution affect our enjoyment of this stopover. We also take the ferry and visit Itaparica, the very large island (joined to the main land by a small strip of land) across the bay from Salvador.

19/10/06–25/10/06

The crew of *Celtic Spirit* rose early on the morning of the 19th to prepare to leave Salvador. A visit to the Port Captain's office completed the exit formalities. It was a hot day but big black clouds hung in the sky and we felt a few drops of rain as we left the bay, passing by Salvador's New-York-style skyline with the high-rise buildings of its financial district. This first day's sail saw our first record of 201 miles in 24 hours averaging 8.37 knots.

Our weather forecast system had predicted that the winds would decrease and move around to the south. This shift was slowly taking place. By the end of our second day the wind had come around in our face and was blowing 25 knots. The seas became confused and heaped. We tacked back and forth for the next two days. On our second night out, winds increased to 36 knots and around 0300 a loud tearing noise was heard. We had ripped our reefed mainsail right up the middle and lost two battens in the process. This would slow us down but at least we had the mizzen to compensate.

Our progress was slow as we tacked out to avoid the Abrolhos Archipelago that we had hoped to visit. Unfortunately due to the wind direction, our time of arrival and the dangerous coral reefs surrounding the islands we reluctantly sailed on. These islands are Brazil's biggest concentration of offshore coral reefs and the best diving and snorkelling spot on the coast. In addition, whales come from Antarctica to breed in the warm waters of this archipelago. As we passed the archipelago to the south we spotted many whales, though mostly in the distance. Not long after passing Abrolhos we headed into an area dotted with oil rigs so one had to be alert at night. As we had missed Abrolhos Islands we decided to go into Buzios, an anchorage approximately 120 miles north of Rio de Janerio. This is a beautiful small town made famous by Brigitte Bardot years ago when she stayed there with her Brazilian boyfriend. We dropped anchor outside the yacht club, late Clube de Buzios, as darkness was falling. This yacht club is quite exclusive and beautifully maintained.

While the centre of town is a little touristy we preferred to hang out closer to the yacht club where it was quieter and so we made ourselves comfortable in a restaurant, making friends with the owner along with other locals. Sliders restaurant is owned by an American originally from Michigan and who produces the best food in the town. We had heard from other sailors in Salvador that the marina

Clockwise from above:
The coast of Buzios comes into view. / A squall hits during the night. / The church tower on the top of the hill. / Sliders restaurant next to the Yacht Club in Buzios.

in Rio was not very secure and the private and exclusive yacht club was the place to go but that one needed an invitation to stay there. Ken, the owner of the restaurant, offered to help by talking to the manager of Buzios Yacht Club and shortly afterwards an invitation was secured for the very exclusive late Clube do Rio de Janeiro, our next port of call. Six days after leaving Salvador we arrived 0500 at Rio de Janeiro's beautiful yacht club which had all the facilities of a five star hotel including its own swimming pool, bank, chandlers, barbers, internet rooms and taxis. As we were guests of the club there was no cost to us for these excellent facilities.

Left: *(from top) Statues of fisherman in the water surrounded by fishing boats some of them old and traditional.* | ***Top and left:*** *The view across to the less touristy part of Buzios.*

Rio de Janeiro

Known as* cidade maravilhosa *or the marvellous city, Rio de Janeiro is vibrant and exciting, dramatically set between mountains, rainforests, beaches and sea. Densely populated, it is full of friendly, easy-going people who enjoy life to the rhythm of Samba music and dancing.

26/10/06–09/11/06

Clearing formalities into Rio was similar to that of Salvador and took almost a full day once again. With our invite to stay at the late Clube Rio de Janerio, *Celtic Spirit* spent her two weeks in Rio at anchor in Botafogo Bay, looked over on one side by the Sugar Loaf and by Christ the Redeemer on the other. The club is situated in Urca, a quiet, leafy and mostly residential area. With the beaches of Copacabana, Ipanema and Leblon to the south and the city centre and its suburbs to the north we were well situated to get just about everywhere in Rio. There was a taxi rank right outside the door of the club and an excellent bus and metro service nearby. The driving in Rio had some of the crew hanging on with white knuckles as the cabs sped through the traffic, ignoring safe driving distances and red lights! Red traffic lights in Rio are considered a safety suggestion at best.

The late Clube itself was fantastic. The crew made good use of the library's computers and wireless internet connection, the bar (which served the best Caipirinihas in town) and the water taxis (our favourite was called Cocoraco), which would bring crew back at various hours of the night, sometimes dropping off crew after a night out while collecting other crew setting off for some sightseeing first thing in the morning! We were also able to get our sails repaired here with North Sails who did an excellent job.

Our go-slow approach to Rio de Janeiro in order to arrive inside the bay with some daylight, adds to the anticipation of seeing this famous city for the first time.

Michiel's log entry

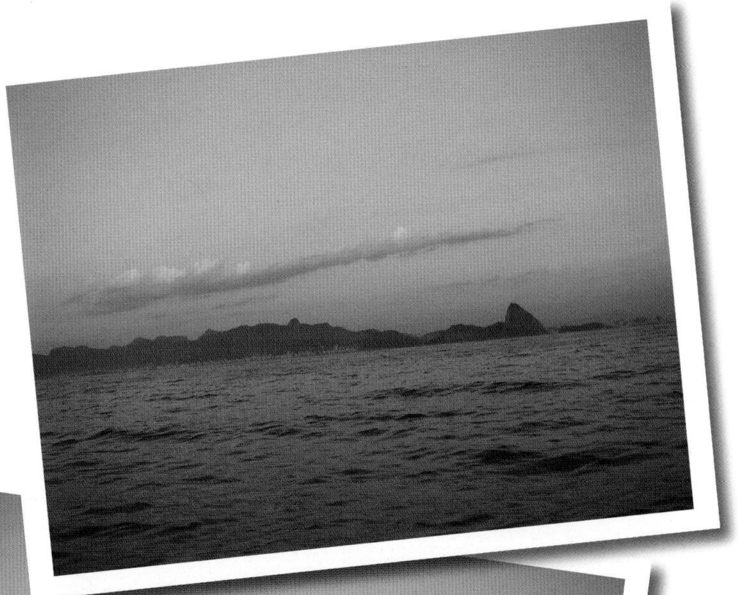

Opposite page:
View from the Corcovado across Rio's Flamengo, Botofogo and Urca districts to the Sugar Loaf and Guanbarra Bay. /
Above: *(top) The coastline of Rio de Janiero comes into view as the sun comes up.* / *(bottom) The Pão de Açúcar (Sugar Loaf) in the foreground and Corcovado (with the statue of Christ the Redeemer on top) in the background.*

Clockwise from top left: *Iate Club Rio de Janeiro. / The club's water taxi on its return from* Celtic Spirit *(in the background). / View from the Sugar Loaf across Botofogo Bay to the Corcovado which is covered in cloud (the yacht club to the bottom right). / The view across to Flamengo with* Celtic Spirit *in the middle of the bay, the furthermost boat out from the club.*

'... seven, eight. Samba backwards. Remember more movement the hips. One, two, three. One, two, three. One, two, three.' It's samba class and stiff like a Swede my hips are moving about as much as a well-planted light post on a still spring day. Luis, the teacher that has danced since the day he was born, thinks I need more lessons. Samba is fun but hard work. For me to reach the most basic level of competence would take years of full-on kamikaze training. So I guess I have to settle for charmingly, foreign half-measures.

JohnJohn's diary entry

Clockwise from right: *From the top of the Sugar Loaf looking down on the little beach at Vermelha and across to the long stretch of Leme and Copacabana beaches – Ipanema is further south. / Copacabana beach at sunset. / A cable car ride brings one to the top of Pão de Açúcar (Sugar Loaf). / The Sugar Loaf. / The view we had from the boat across to Urca overlooked by the Sugar Loaf.*

Clockwise from top left: *A motorbike-taxi makes its way through the busy streets of Rochina. / Across the roof tops sit the blue water drums. / All the way up the hillside, one dwelling built on top of another.*

While some crew returned to see family, those left in Rio did their best to become locals. Samba lessons at the well-known Carlinhos de Jesus School of Samba were the order of the day. Their teacher was Luis Claudio who, apart from being brilliant, remained patient while all did their best to get their feet into the samba rhythm. On leaving, Luis was promised that 'exercise, practise and more movement the hips' would continue!

Everyday at least one Caipiriniha had to be consumed and soon the most essential items in the shopping bag were a bottle of Cachaca and limes. Using these key ingredients, cut the small limes into quarters, add sugar, ice cubes and then the Cachaca. This is a high proof alcohol made from sugar cane and many bars and restaurants have whole menus devoted to the many brands that are available.

The crew explored Rio from Leblon and Ipanema to Santa Teresa and Centro by day and by night. They went to the beach, the cinema,

Clockwise from top left: *The narrow streets of Rochina – a tangle of wires crisscrosses from one side of the street to the other. / Ansis eating acai / Paulo and Michiel in the shop where we have our first taste of acai. / Paulo, Janet and Ansis at the very top of Rochina. / JohnJohn and Michiel in Temos, the best restaurant in Rochina.*

museums, art galleries, markets, restaurants, pubs, clubs and made friends with the Cariocas (the name given to the people of Rio). They went up the Sugar Loaf from where there was a good view of the boat and took two tours, one to a *favela* (a slum) and one to the Corcovado (Christ the Redeemer statue).

Very yummy, lovely jubly stuff. Smashed ice with acai berries.
Ansis describes acai

The highlight of our visit to Rio was meeting Paulo Amendoim, a former president of the residents' association of Rio's largest *favela*, Rochina. He is also involved in its child-care project. Rochina has more than 127,000 inhabitants and is one of the most developed slums having obtained the status of *bairro* (district). Paulo is a wonderful man who is obviously loved and respected by all from young to old. He seemed to know everyone as we walked up through the *favela* which is built precariously all the way up the hillside. He brought us for some delicious acai, made from the Amazononian fruit of the same name. We each chose a different topping for what can best be described as a smoothie so thick and cold you need to eat it. From the top of the *favela* we got motorbike cab rides back to the bottom. This was a special and amazing experience, nipping in and out between the buses and cars amongst the gridlocked traffic snaking up the hillside.

It was all smiles and thumbs up - "Tudo bem!" Even the fifteen year old, wearing full arm lizard tattoo and M16 with silver duct tape around the clip, guarding the neighbourhood against rival gangs, said hi.
JohnJohn's diary entry

Rochina is a big and lively place. While the people who live there have very little they are happy and a community spirit is evident.

Our tour of the Corcovado was led by Dolores Leao who collected us in a big metallic-green jeep. From the yacht club we drove up through the Tijuca forest, everyone feeling the chill as we got higher. Dolores was wonderful, filling us with information on the city as well as the statue. Our trip back took us through Santa Teresa, past the house of Ronnie Biggs, the famous British train robber, and through Centro to the new cathedral with its strange cone shape. Dolores is a bright and bubbly person who also makes very good Cachaca. We were given a bottle of it to sample.

Brazilians love their music and dancing. There are plenty of places to go for live samba music and dancing including restaurants where you pay a cover charge for the music, which it is well worth it. Our favourite spots were Severyna in Laranjeiras, Carioca da Gema in Lapa and a couple of places in Santa Teresa.

Above: *A monkey in the Tajuca forest. | **Left:** (clockwise from bottom) Christ the Redeemer from different points of view – back and front. | Christ the Redeemer. | Dolores filling us with information on Rio as we drive up to the Corcovado. | Christ the Redeemer on top of the Corcovado amid the Tajuca Forest.*

Clockwise from top left: *Ronny Biggs' house in Santa Teresa. / The cathedral with its very modern design. / Michiel's sketch of Santa Helena. / We make friends from Peru, Colombia and Argentina in Carioca de Gemma. / The tram that runs through Santa Teresa.*

A British sailor we met in Salvador recommended we avoid Rio but we have to say it is not to be missed. However, we will be taking his advice to visit Parati, which is an 80 mile sail further along the coast where we hope to meet with the skipper of *Paratii 2*, a famous expedition yacht in Brazil. There, two Brazilian crew will join us for the next leg of our journey south. We have heard it is very, very beautiful!

09/11/06–12/11/06

Celtic Spirit departed Rio on Thursday evening 8 November. We motored out of Baia de Guanabara and headed south, passing the long stretches of Copacabana, Ipanema and Leblon beaches where the wind picked up a little and we had a couple of close encounters with fishing boats and their nets.

In the early hours of the following morning we were making our way into Baia da Parati, which is situated to the southwest of Baia da Ilha Grande, the jewel of the south Brazilian coastline with 365 tropical islands, one for each day of the year. Not only is it magnificently beautiful but it is a cruising paradise with many safe anchorages. By 0930 we were anchored just off Marina Engenho, which belongs to Amyr Klink who has his boat *Paratii 2* berthed there. This is a 90-foot aluminium boat built specifically to sail to Antarctica and in which he has circumnavigated the blue continent. It has a laden weight of 100 tonnes and carries 33,000 litres of fuel and 3,000 litres of water. It has two unstayed masts with a boom sail configuration. She is built for pure practicality and not for aesthetics. However, she is a fine-looking vessel and our crew wandered around her in awe. Although her owner was not in Parati at the time, we met her skipper Fabio who graciously showed us around and answered our many questions.

Top and bottom (from left): *Tropical Parati with the mountains in the background and palm trees, church and tourist ferries in the foreground. / Fishing boats and schooners for hire by tourists line the pier in Parati.*

Clockwise from bottom left: *The cobbled streets of Parati washed clean at high tide. / The asymmetrical church in Parati. / A local man makes colourful wooden boats to sell as souvenirs. / As we speed away in the dinghy we leave behind Parati set below tropical mountains full of scenic waterfalls.*

Clockwise from above: *Michiel's drawing of* Paratii 2. / Paratii 2 *is the silver-hulled boat in the middle of the three boats.* / *Amyir Klinks Marina Engenho where* Paratii 2 *is berthed.* / *The cockpit of* Paratii 2. / *The view along her decks.* / *Our skipper Michael and Fabio the skipper of* Paratii 2.

Parati itself is a beautiful town nestled beneath the surrounding mountains. It is one of the oldest Brazilian cities and is a national monument because the buildings are of a unique colonial architecture and are very well kept. The streets are closed to vehicular traffic and pedestrians wander along their uneven cobblestones which are washed clean at high tide by water that comes through from the harbour. This town is a favourite holiday spot for Brazilians as well as Europeans and is colourful and lively. It is also renowned for its excellent Cachaca.

Our Brazilian crew, Fabrizio and Igor, joined us on the second day here and immediately became part of the *Celtic Spirit* family. Apart from being excellent sailors, their local knowledge and help with both the Portuguese and Spanish languages was extremely useful. In the evening we weighed anchor and motored over to a tiny island about two miles away, Ilha Rasa, where we had booked the restaurant for dinner. We had a beautiful meal in a beautiful setting before returning to the boat for a bit of music, chat and Cachaca drinking. *Celtic Spirit's* next destination is Uruguay.

Far left (top and bottom): *The island of Ilha Rosa and its restaurant. / Palm fringed beach. /* ***Centre (from top) and above:*** *Michiel drinks from a coconut. / Igor cuts open a coconut. / Ansis and Igor walking along a palm fringed beach with Marina Engenho in the background. / Ansis and Igor with a hand of bananas. /* ***Above:*** *We pass a rocky island on our way out of Baia da Parati.*

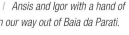

Brazil to Argentina

After checking out of Brazil we head to Punte del Este in Uruguay. From there we have a brief stop in Mar del Plata, Argentina before heading on to Ushuaia. On our way to Ushuaia at the bottom of Argentina we sail from latitude 30° through the Roaring Forties and Furious Fifties stopping in three countries on the way.

Opposite page: *Reeling in the biggest fish to be caught so far.*

13/11/06–18/11/06

For two days after leaving Parati we had good wind of over 20 knots increasing to 30 knots, which made for great sailing under reefed genny, main and mizzen. Over the following days the wind came around to the northeast, which meant we could pole out the genoa and staysail. In our first twenty-four hours we averaged 197 miles at 8.2 knots and in our second twenty-four hours we averaged 199 miles at 8.3 knots. After just three days' sailing we had covered just over 600 miles. This has been our best speed and distance so far. Along this coastline there is plenty of shipping and fishing vessels so watches were always busy.

It seems our fishing has improved. A large dorade was caught whilst doing over 9 knots much to the delight of the crew as it made a delicious dinner. Two days later we caught an even larger dorade measuring 107 cm long, our biggest catch ever, followed by a large sun fish! It was clear that fish was to feature on our menu over the coming days.

Cooked four portions of today's dorado in the oven á la provencale. Meal for eight. Still two meals in this magnificent fish. Dolphins playing at the bow at sunset. Lots of cirrus clouds later in the day, temp dropping.

Michiel's diary entry

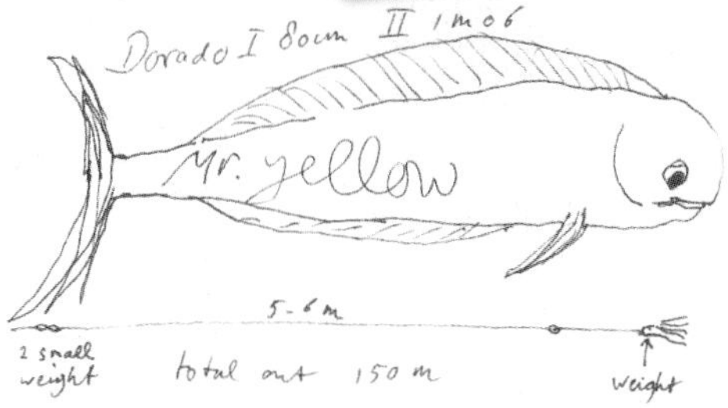

Clockwise from below: *Dorade in the net. | Michiel proudly holds up his fish – over 1 m long. | Dorade chopped up and ready for cooking. | Michiel's drawing of his catch, Mr Yellow.*

In order to leave Brazil one has to clear out at a chosen port. This we did at Rio Grande. Approaching Rio Grande during the dark hours of night was challenging. Lights began appearing on the horizon and at first glance were mistaken for lights on shore, however, closer inspection revealed they were, in fact, a line of fishing boats. As we sailed closer, we tracked them on the radar counting a total of twenty-seven boats. There were ten within 3 miles and seven within 2 miles of us at one stage.

Arriving in Rio Grande in the early hours of the morning we dropped anchor in the bay outside the entrance to the port in 7 m of water. The wind was blowing a gale and the waters were very rough. During the night the anchor had dragged a kilometre and although we had plenty of sea room this was of some concern. On raising the anchor we noticed that we had bent the shank of our 80 kg Bruce slightly. The following morning we contacted port control and arranged to anchor inside the entrance. They were kind enough to send a boat out to collect us and arranged a car to drive us to the police station and Port Captain's office in order to get all our paperwork sorted out. Afterwards we were delivered back to the boat. Having officially cleared out of Brazil we again weighed anchor and headed off in the direction of Punte del Este, Uruguay's most popular holiday resort.

21/11/06–02/12/06

We intended visiting Montevideo, Uruguay but our draft restricted this so we spent a few days in Punta del Este approximately 100 miles east. Although this is a well known holiday resort with a scenic coast and fine beaches and popular amongst wealthy South Americans we found it to be without character so we set sail for Mar del Plata some 300 miles away where we hoped to refuel for the long leg to the bottom of the South American continent. Mar del Plata itself is a big place laid out on a grid system. We were now in Argentina and once again in a new country and had the usual formalities to deal with. As we only intended staying long enough to refuel with this country's cheap diesel we used a clearing agent to

Below (top and bottom): *Janet checks through all our passports and paperwork. / Port Control brings the skipper in to Rio Grande to clear out. /* ***Right (top and bottom):*** *Port Control at the pier in Rio Grande. / The Brazilian flag comes down and the Uruguayan flag goes up as we sail from one country to the next.*

Woke up to 37 knots' wind and the boat dragging anchor. In ten minutes it dragged 120 m!

Skipper's log entry

URUGUAY

Left: *(top and bottom) Ansis and Igor bring lines ashore and tie up* Celtic Spirit *in Punte del Este.* / ***Centre:*** *(top and bottom) The sky-line of Punte del Este behind the boats in the harbour.* / *The streets of Punte del Este.* / ***Right:*** *(top and bottom) JohnJohn, looking Swedish, stands next to one of the many old cars to be found in South America.* / *The hand sculpture on the beach at Punte del Este.*

process our paperwork as quickly as possible. However, the clearance in and out including special customs' clearance to take on diesel still took twenty-four hours. The following morning we were on our way again, motor-sailing in light winds. After a day, the wind shifted to our stern and we decided to drop our large mainsail in favour of poling out our two headsails. Without warning, and in the middle of our sail changes, the wind increased to over 40 knots. In less than an hour it had dropped off again and after a frustrating day of trying to track the wind we were resigned to motor-sailing once again.

Each day that followed was sunny and beautiful but the air and sea temperatures were dropping. Thermals, hats, gloves and boots began making an appearance. For the first time we saw albatross. We identified one of them as the royal and another as the wandering albatross. They followed us, flying by in an impressive display, landing gracefully on the water where they would sit for a while and then catch up with us later again. We had now entered the roaring forties. Winds increased but were still on the nose. Speed was dismal. According to our weather forecast the wind was due to increase and come around to the north. By the following morning the wind had increased and was behind us, 25 to 35 knots. We poled out the genny and staysail. The seas were building. Waves of at least 5 m came piling down towards the boat, some swiping at us from the side. One deposited itself into the cockpit on top of a crewmember who was on watch. Luckily, the companionway doors were closed or there would have been a flood down below. Albatrosses and petrels continued to patrol the sea around the boat, flying up and down, skimming over the surface of the waves as they rose and fell, keeping us company. Every day showed a marked difference in temperature, which was now down to around 12 °C. It was sunny but cold while the water temperature was falling at a rate of 1 °C each day.

The wind continually went up and down as we constantly worked our sails, moving around to the southwest and onto a beat again. We dropped

Clockwise from top right: *Sea lions in the harbour. / Sharing the fisherman's spoils with the Gulls. / Hanging out on the harbour wall.*

Clockwise from top left: *Rainbow on the horizon. / The evening sky. / An albatross takes a rest. / A sky full of birds following* Celtic Spirit. ***Right:*** *Michiel's drawings of all the birds we have following us.*

the mizzen and put up a fully-reefed mainsail together with a reefed genny. This would give us better stability and took us almost an hour as it was not easy while we slammed into the oncoming waves. The wind increased to 32 knots and remained consistently between 28 and 32 knots all day. The sea state was somewhat rough with its irregular wave pattern making life down below a little like a washing machine and the galley a tough place to work. We were hoping for a wind shift that would enable us to head in a more southwesterly direction as we were heading directly south and for the Falkland Islands! We needed to move further to the west so that we could make the gap at the toe of Argentina and avoid being blown on to the Falklands. After a further two days the wind moved around to the north and we were finally able to move more to the southwest and head in a better direction. The wind was now behind us at 30-plus knots as we moved into

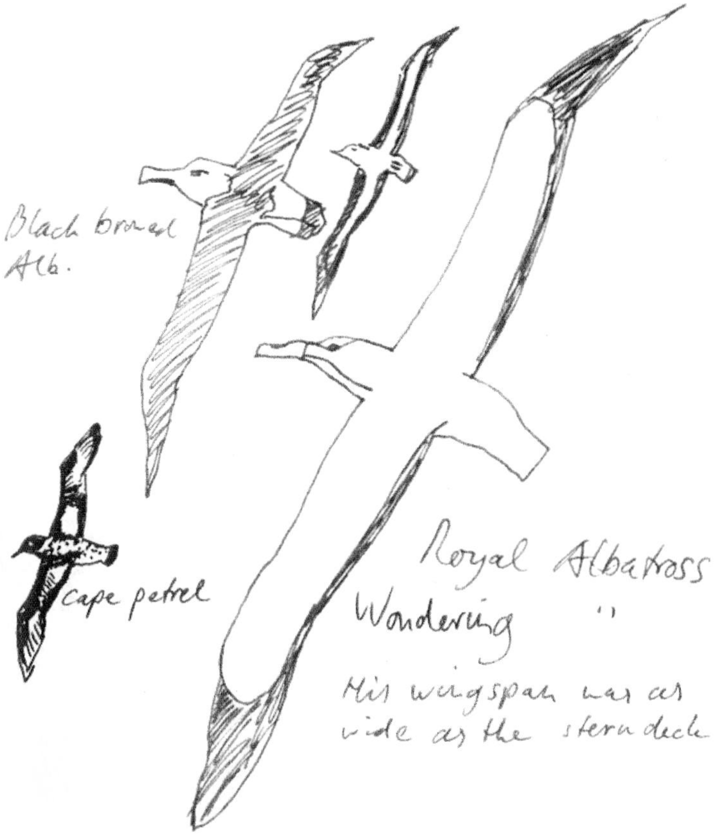

a good position to descend down on the gap between Tierra del Fuego and Isla de la Estados. Seas were up to 7 m but progress was good and exciting as we surfed down waves at up to 12 knots.

We arrived at Estrecho de la Maire, the expanse of water between Tierra del Fuego and Isla de la Estados, on Friday 1 December. The passage up the Beagle Canal was carefully planned with waypoints and estimated times of arrival at each of these as we would be making our way up here during the night. This would make it easier to navigate. The watch system was changed for this last part of the journey. Crew were divided into two teams. First watch would cover the first section of the canal and the second watch the rest and more tricky section. It was a cold night that did not get fully dark. We encountered a cruise liner but very little other traffic and all in all it was a relatively straightforward passage although winds were over 25 knots and currents were strong at times. The scenery was beautiful as we sailed up the Beagle Canal with its surrounding snow- and ice-capped mountains. After 1,500 miles and nearly ten days at sea we arrived in Ushuaia. We anchored off and as usual a dinghy party went ashore to check depths and deal with formalities. The crew on the boats at the pontoon were most helpful and moved around some of the boats to fit us in. Depth was critical and we would depend on *Celtic Spirit's* ability to sink into the mud by up to half a metre at low water. We knew it would be difficult to come alongside into a tight spot with strong winds blowing us off and very little ability to manoeuvre due to the shallow water. We circled for a while waiting for a temporary lull in the strong wind and when it dropped to 20 knots we made a dash for our spot. A large crowd from the pontoon was watching (some in fear) as our new-found friends helped us to tie up without fuss or incident. *Celtic Spirit* will spend Christmas and the New Year in Ushuaia with three crew onboard while the others go home for a well-earned break before returning in January for the next part of our exciting voyage to Antarctica.

Right: *(top and bottom) The crew in Mar del Plata. /* Celtic Spirit *tied up in the harbour in Mar del Plata. /* ***Far right and opposite page:*** *Passing between Tierra del Fuego and Isla Estados down Estrecho de la Maire.*

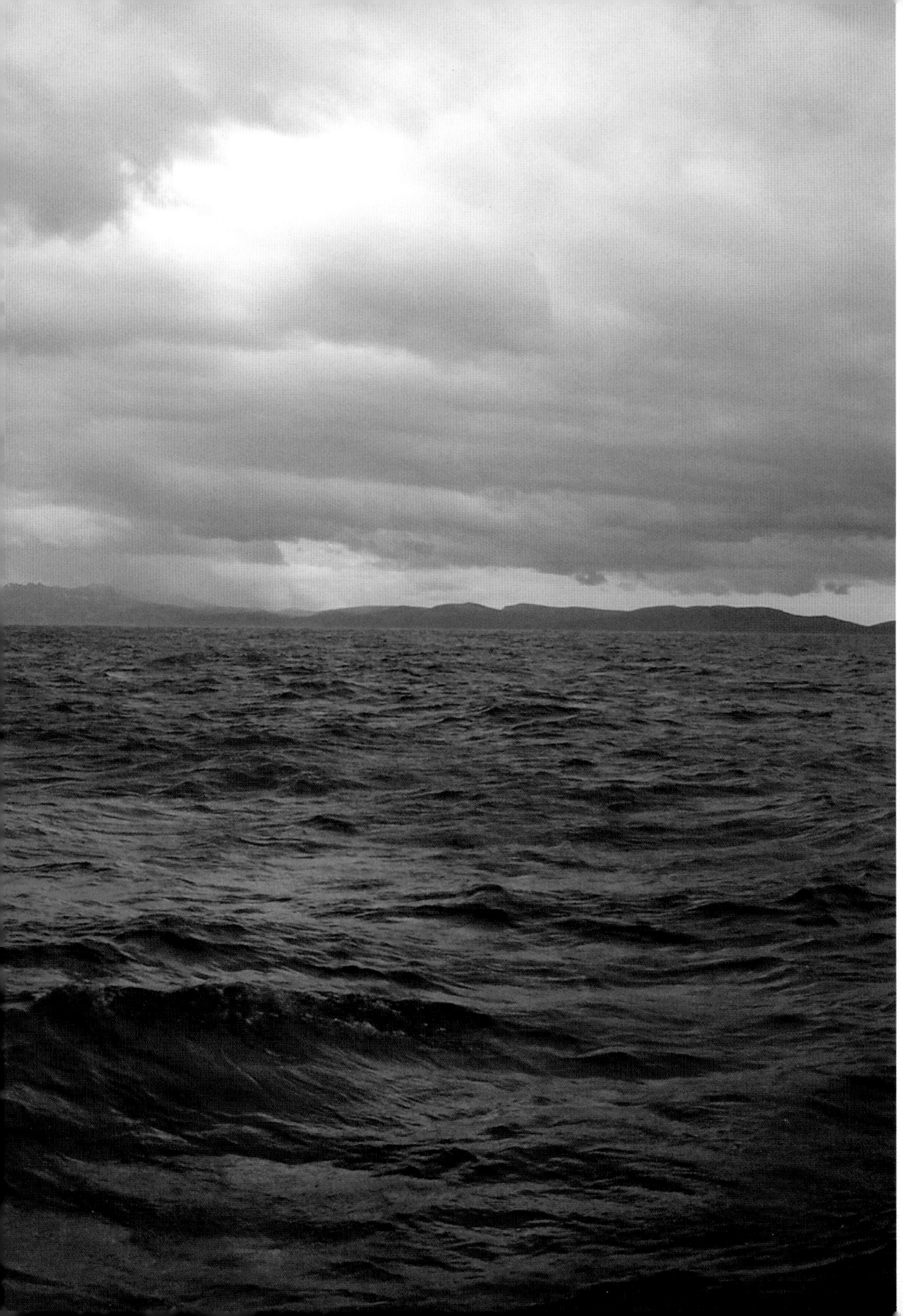

The Southern Ocean

The official demarcation of the Southern Ocean is 40° south latitude. It includes the latitudes nicknamed the Roaring Forties, the Furious Fifties and the Screaming Sixties. It is an area of almost constant high winds and frequent gales. In storms the waves build until they reach almost unimaginable heights. Icebergs and smaller 'growlers' drift through the frigid water. Over the centuries it has been a sailors' graveyard. The wilderness of ice and water are terrible places where nature retains ultimate power.

In the Southern Ocean the fragile lines that connect the sailor to humanity are stretched to the limit.

Skipper's log entry

Ushuaia

Ushuaia, Tierra del Fuego, Argentina. It is a wild and beautiful place, and the base for boats heading to Antarctica. It lies along the Beagle Canal, which separates Argentina from Chile. This is* Celtic Spirit's *home for Christmas and New Year, a break before tackling the Drake Passage and Antarctica.

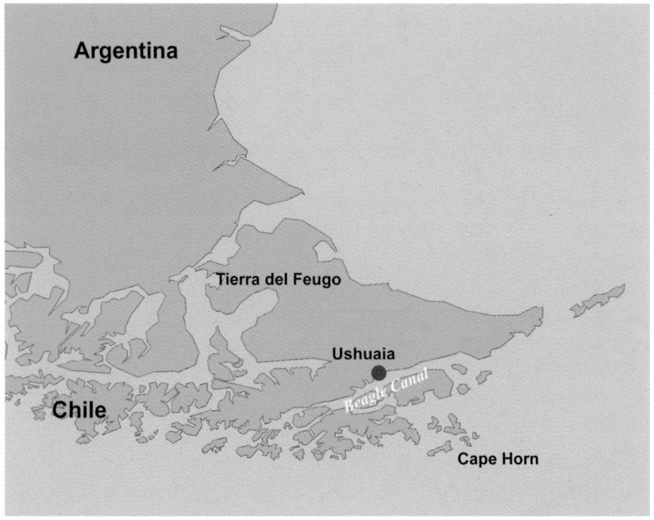

Opposite page: *The boats on the pontoon at AFYSyN, with Ushuaia in the background.* / **Top and bottom:** *Michiel's drawing of the Beagle Canal.* / *The crew on the foredeck the day we arrived in Ushuaia, back: Blayney, Janet, Michael and JohnJohn; front: Michiel and Ansis.*

02/12/06–19/01/07

During the six-week break when some crew returned home, those left on board *Celtic Spirit* enjoyed the experience of getting to know their surroundings in Ushuaia. This is the world's most southern city, with a population of 50,000 people, set below jagged, ice-capped mountains and nestling halfway up the Beagle Canal.

The crew enjoyed getting to know the locals and nightlife of this town at the end of the world. Ansis learned to do the tango, absorbing its art form and music. Others spent time tuning into nature, taking walks along the beaches of the Beagle Canal, visiting Tierra del Fuego National Park and walking in the mountains that make Ushuaia unique.

There were plenty of jobs to be done onboard and work continued in order to prepare the boat for its next and most important leg. The pontoon at Marina AFYSyN is a small but busy one and boats arrive and

On 3 January 2007, having spent a few days in Buenos Aires with blue skies, scorching sun and 40 °C heat, Denis and I flew to Ushuaia to rejoin the crew for the trip to Antarctica. Lashing wind and rain, black skies, threatening wild dark seas and zero temperatures greeted our arrival. The wind whipped the sea into a frenzy as we struggled down the marina laden with sailing gear. We found Celtic Spirit, the hatch flew open and Ansis bounded out to greet us. A warm glow emanated from the interior. A Christmas tree sparkled, Michiel was hovering over a pot of bolognese and JohnJohn was dancing around the saloon. A bottle of wine was produced, the hatch was closed and we enjoyed one of the best meals of the trip. Having finished, we were whisked by taxi to a local hostelry Dreamland where a great night ensued with tango dancing and partaking of the local drink. We woke up the following morning to the most beautiful, stunning views of blue sky and snow-covered mountains bathed in sunlight.

Vera's diary entry

Clockwise from below: *The mountains behind Ushuaia.* / Celtic Spirit *(left) on the pontoon at AFYSyN.* / Celtic Spirit *with her Christmas decorations.*

Clockwise from top left: *Boats on their moorings in front of Ushuaia and its snow-capped peaks in the background. / The view down the Beagle from the road to Ushuaia. / The road to Ushuaia. / Ushuaia. / A view of the pontoon at AFYSyN from the road to Ushuaia with the Beagle Canal in the background. / Another shot of the pontoon, with Ushuaia behind it.*

Clockwise from top right:
Andy and Janet watch and listen as Donnna plays her steel drum on board Zephyrus. / *Michiel plays the violin.* / *JohnJohn on guitar.* / *Ushuaia at night.* / *Donna on guitar.*

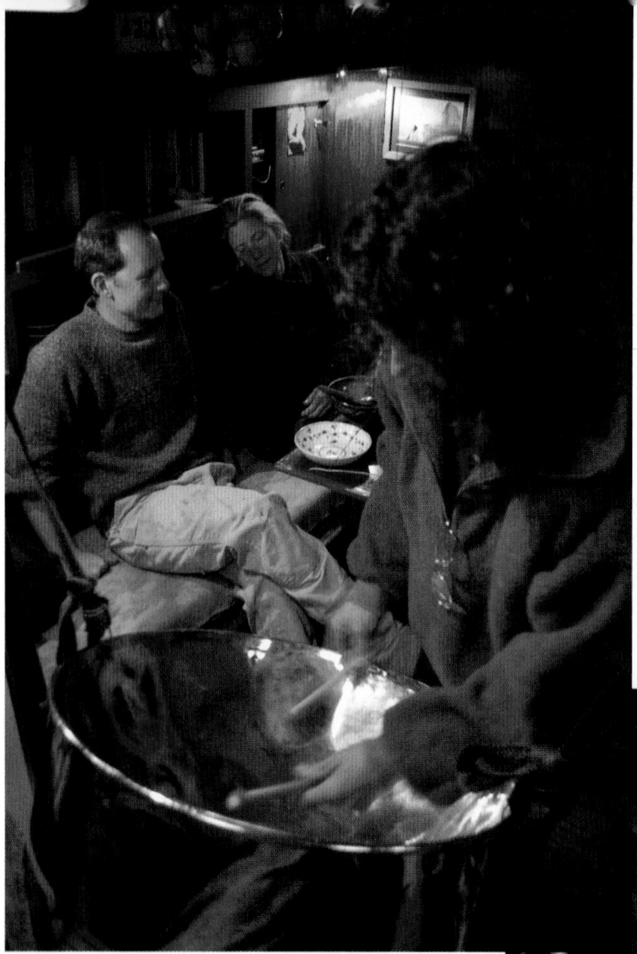

Left: *(top and bottom) An unusual perspective up a tree in the National Park. / San Martin the main street in Ushuaia.*
Clockwise from left: *A view down the Beagle Canal. / Ansis does the Tango with Caroline. / JohnJohn, Ansis and a diver attach the fixed blade propellers. / JohnJohn cleans the propeller before it goes on.*

depart daily, some en route to or from Antarctica. Many of the sailors arriving here have sailed many thousands of miles around the world. There are boats that operate private charter trips to the Antarctic and some are here to explore the Beagle Canal. Amongst those that tied up alongside were *Pelagic,* owned and run by Skip Novak and *Wanderer III*, which used to belong to Eric Hiscock. Meeting the people from the many boats, both the well-known and otherwise, was humbling. These people come from all over the world, from different walks of life and they have vast sailing experience. We were grateful for their willingness to help out and impart knowledge.

We were visited by Mariolina Rolfo and Giorgio Ardrizzi, authors of the very comprehensive Patagonian nautical pilot book, considered to be the definitive authority on the Beagle Canal. Michiel happily spent time speaking Dutch to Eef Willems of *Tooluka* who is full of knowledge on Antarctic waters. We made friends with Jochen and Wolf Kloss of *Santa Maria Austraulis* and regular visitors on board *Celtic Spirit* were our neighbours Andy and Alex of *Zephyrus* as well as Donna Lange who has sailed solo around the world on a 28-foot boat and who kept us entertained with her jamming sessions. Donna was a breath of fresh air, her music and attitude to life will always be remembered. We wish her well and a safe passage home.

Antarctica

In mid-January 2007 we leave the comfort of Ushuaia and set sail for Antarctica and the unknown. To get there we must cross the infamous Drake Passage. Everyone is apprehensive and extremely excited at the same time. What will this crossing be like and what treasures await us along the coast of the blue continent?

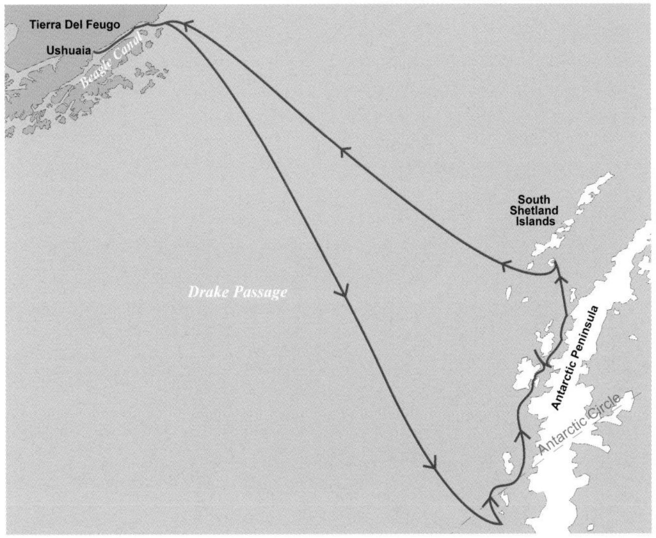

Opposite page and right: Celtic Spirit *crosses the Drake Passage.* | *Mist and fog create an eerie atmosphere as we cross the Antarctic Convergence Zone.*

USHUAIA to the ANTARCTIC CIRCLE

19/01/07

Two days were spent provisioning, stowing, fixing and repairing the last things on the never-ending list of boat maintenance, including installing a new weather system. This system, which all boats that venture into Ushuaia seem to acquire, gives live aerial photos of the region and also has a tracking feature. We had taken up a mooring in the bay so that we could leave as soon as we were ready and not be restricted by the tide at the pontoon. It was late afternoon by the time we set out with little wind and under engine. On advice given to the skipper it was decided not to go into Puerto Williams and instead head straight for the Antarctic. Although it saved time on checking in and out procedures it meant that we had to remain in Argentinean waters en route south to Antarctica and could not stray into the southern part of the Beagle Canal, which is controlled by Chile.

20/01/07

The wind so far has stayed light and below 10 knots. This morning was slightly foggy but it soon cleared and has been sunny all day. Although there is a nip in the air it is relatively warm. We have had dolphins with us in the early hours of this morning and albatrosses during the day. The new and fixed blade propellers that were fitted before setting out on this leg of our journey are slower than the folding props, so we have averaged 142 miles in 24 hours. These propellers 'sing' adding to the eerie atmosphere as we cross the flat calm of the Drake. It is only after our voyage that we find out that the singing noise is due to the incorrect pitch of the propellers, an error in calculation that was made when the props were manufactured.

Holes litter
my wardrobe. The wet gear is patched
up with the same white goo that seals your
kitchen sink to the wall. Forgot to buy
toothpaste. But I'm going to Antarctica
just the same. This is as sweet as it gets.
JohnJohn's diary entry

21/01/07

During the early hours of this morning a bright light with long tail was seen in the sky. It is the comet McNaught, which is said to have been the brightest comet seen for thirty years. Today has brought us mostly fog that threatened to clear but did not. While the wind remains light and under 10 knots the sea rises and falls in a gentle swell. Progress under both engines is still slow but good; in 24 hours we travel 160 miles at an average of 6.6 knots. The temperature dropped significantly during this afternoon and it is apparent that we have now entered the Antarctic Convergence Zone. This is a zone, sometimes marked by localised fog and mist, where the warm, more saline surface currents coming south from the tropics meet the cold, denser and mainly non-saline waters moving north from the Antarctic. Here the waters are rich with plankton, which nourishes large numbers of sea birds and sea mammals.

22/01/07

Still under engine and averaging 6.6 knots, we have covered 168 miles. The swell has gone and the wind is hanging around 10 knots and from behind. The water temperature is now down to 2 °C and the outside air temperature is 8 °C. Everyone has cold feet despite wearing warm socks and boots. Although this is not the weather we had expected we are all enjoying the calm while it lasts. We discover that using the water maker brings good results due to the low salinity of the water here. The plan is to sail down to Crystal Sound and over the Antarctic Circle although there are no detailed charts of this area.

23/01/07

The nights now are not fully dark and the water temperature is down to 1.2 °C. A sooty albatross is seen flying near to the boat and a whale spout is also seen a short distance away.

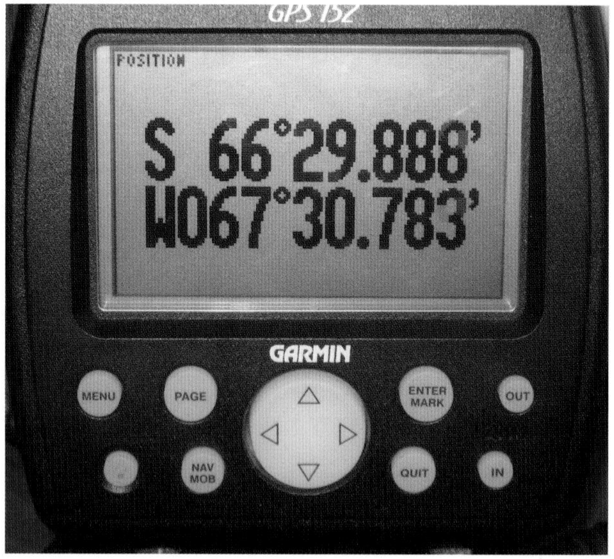

Clockwise from top left: *Antarctic circle ahoy! Ansis and Blayney point to the imaginary line, our Irish flag flies proudly in the background. / Our GPS reading at the Antarctic Circle. / We encounter our first bits of ice, both big and small.*

Seventeen hours 'til we start weaving our way through the islands. Will be exciting. Much of the charts look plain and simply only half done. Dotted lines indicating guesses, depth contours ending abruptly for lack of information, big areas are marked 'unsurveyed', blank as the pages of a sketchbook. As if someone went to lunch halfway through and never came back.

JohnJohn's diary entry

24/01/07

Icebergs are seen around 0800 this morning and land becomes visible from 1000. The water is full of growlers and bergy bits with wind up to 30 knots at times. A very lumpy and confused sea makes it difficult to distinguish between ice and white horses. At around 1700 we crossed the Antarctic Circle and we celebrated with some champagne. As we entered Crystal Sound the amount of brash ice causes us to turn around and head north to find an anchorage. We had heard of a place at 66°04′ where good shelter could be obtained. Suitable anchorages and safe havens are difficult to come by and in many cases are closely guarded secrets. The friends we had made in Ushuaia were seasoned Antarctic sailors and they passed on invaluable information on the Antarctic Peninsula. Mutton Cove was one of these safe havens and was to be our first landfall in six days.

Clockwise from top left: *Iceberg ahead! / Full Musto gear, ski googles and thick gloves keep out the cold. / Antarctica ahead of us. / Janet, Vera and Blayney wrapped up warm. / Antarctica behind us. / Icebergs with the majestic peaks of Antarctica mainland behind.*

MUTTON COVE

25/01/07

En route to Mutton Cove (66° S), we have a beautiful calm night with a red sky stretching across the horizon. We arrive outside Mutton Cove early in the morning. It is misty and cold, and there are plenty of bergy bits around. The air is calm and quiet, the scenery breath-takingly beautiful. We pass blue-eyed Antarctic shags perched on the rock face. The entrance to Mutton Cove is blocked by icebergs. While we breakfast on hot porridge the icebergs slowly drift off, opening a gap for us to proceed into this small well-sheltered cove. We tie up in mid-channel with two lines from the bow and two lines from the stern tied on either side to the shore.

The crew is excited and eager to explore. We take the dinghy to shore and finally set foot on Antarctic soil. We climb the hills around our safe haven, feeling like explorers setting foot on land that has never been explored before. There is no sign of civilisation here. It is wonderful, magical and remote.

At the top of the ice-covered cliffs the skuas squawk and attack, angrily warding us off in defence of their young. From here we can see that all the bays surrounding us are filled with icebergs. Every now and then we can hear one calving with a thundering crash into the sea. The sound transports across the still air. Michiel plays his mandolin and its distinctive sound makes its way up from the boat, filling the air with a brand new composition. We stay in this magical cove for the night and celebrate our first landfall in six days with wine and a lovely dinner.

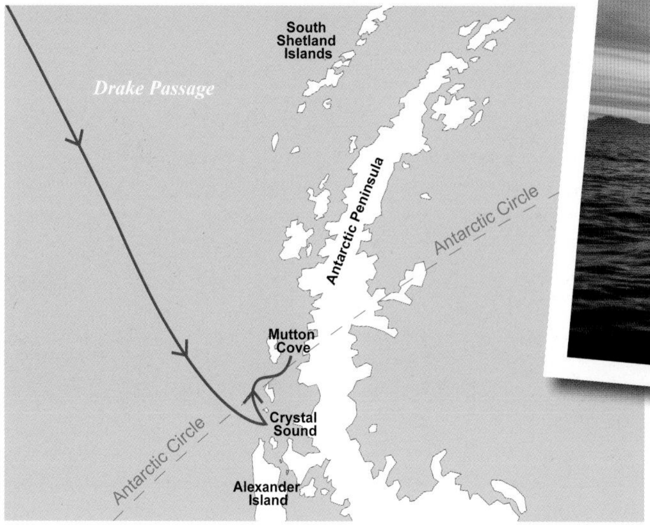

At anchor outside Mutton Cove, awaiting some icebergs to slowly drift away from the entrance, we make a brave attempt to push a moving growler away from the boat by using our dinghy. It catches the stern and cuts a deep groove into the paintwork.

Skipper's log entry

Opposite page: *The icy scenery of Mutton Cove.* | **Top left:** *More ice and fog surrounds us.* | **Above:** *Sunrise as we approach Mutton Cove.*

Left: *(top) The entrance to Mutton Cove.* / *(middle and bottom) Water, ice and cloud cover as far as the eye can see.* / ***Above:*** *Entering Mutton Cove.*
Opposite page: *(clockwise from left)* Celtic Spirit *safely tied up in Mutton Cove.* / *Ansis, Blayney, Michael, Denis and JohnJohn: Antarctic explorers.* / *The view of the surrounding bay from the top of the cliffs.* / *Michiel's drawing of Mutton Cove.*

Mutton Cove: having crossed the Antarctic Circle our first mooring was in this tiny cove. Celtic Spirit lay enclosed, surrounded by snow-capped peaks bathed in sunlight, rolling snow-covered hills and gaunt black rocks etched sharply against virgin snow. Skuas swooping down to protect their territory, icebergs calving – whoosh – and then silence, a timeless, beautiful wilderness.

Vera's diary entry

Clockwise from right: *Our skipper and skuas.* | *JohnJohn takes the dinghy ashore from* Celtic Spirit *where she is tied up in Mutton Cove.* | Celtic Spirit's *mast sticks up out of Mutton Cove.* | *Snow angel.* | *Antarctic Shags.*

Clockwise from top left: *Chinstrap penguins. / Ansis, JohnJohn and Blayney walking on top of the ridge. / Our snowman dressed in Ansis's hat, Denis's glasses with eyes, nose and buttons made of shells left by kelp gulls. / An iceberg in the bay outside Mutton Cove. /* Celtic Spirit *from the water in Mutton Cove.*

VERNADSKY

26/01/07

This morning *Celtic Spirit* left Mutton Cove to head for Vernadsky, the Ukrainian base on Galindez Island, which was known as Faraday until it was transferred from the British for £1 in 1991. The bay is a landscape scattered with ice sculptures of various shapes and sizes. We pick our way carefully through the pieces, avoiding the black ice, which was more difficult to see. Perched on top of a small iceberg were two Adelie penguins and on another, seals reclined. We arrived into Stella Creek at Vernadsky to find *Santa Maria Australis* and *Vaihere* rafted together. Again, tying up to the shore was the only method to moor. It was nice to see people we had met in Ushuaia again. Ansis made contact with the base because he was able to speak Russian to them. They extended a warm welcome and invited us to visit the next day.

27/01/07

Early this morning the two boats next to us left, leaving us alone in the cove, so we explored the surrounding area. Skuas dive-bombed us but we soon discovered that if you ducked to avoid them the next time around they would aim lower. Holding something above our heads like a glove or a stick

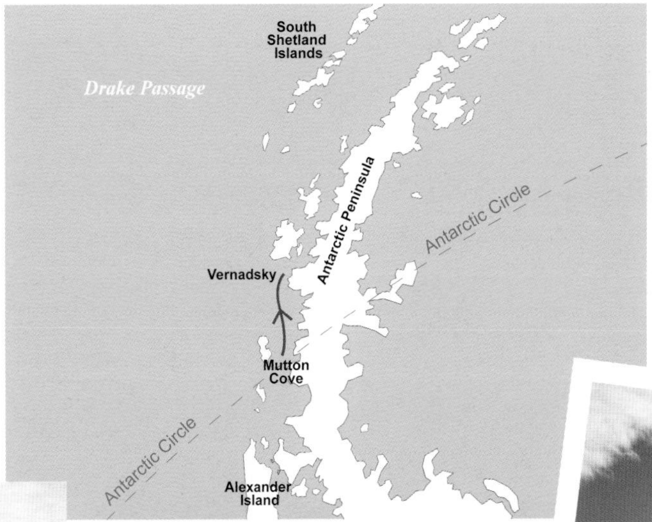

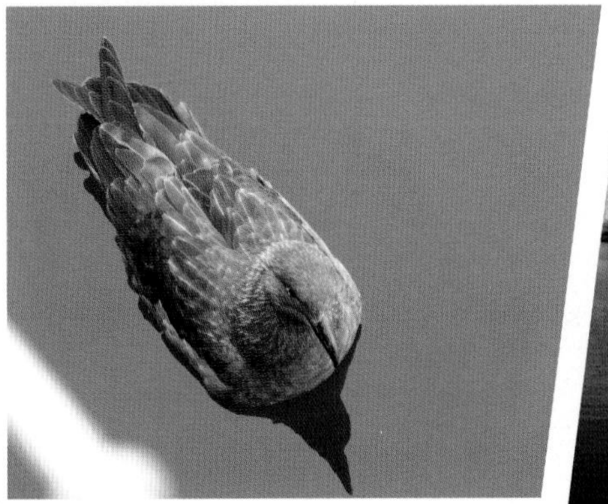

Opposite page: *Vernadsky Base.* / ***Left:*** Celtic Spirit *alone in Stella Creek.* / ***Above:*** *A skua on the still waters of Stella Creek.* / Celtic Spirit *with lines ashore in Stella Creek.*

kept the skuas aiming higher than our heads. A couple of the personnel from the base came over and took the crew out in their Zodiac to see icebergs and seals in the surrounding area. They also gave us the key to Wordie House, a museum and old base station that shows how the researchers used to live. Here we found the visitors' book, which had signatures from Peter Blake and his crew who were there in 2001. He was tragically killed later that year aboard his boat in the Amazon. We went back to the boat for dinner and then over to the base for 2100 where we were taken on a guided tour. Here, they research storms in the ionosphere and other scientific 'stuff' that none of us could comprehend. After the tour we were invited up to the bar for some of their local vodka and where it is custom for women visitors to hand over their bras. They have a collection of all shapes and sizes behind the bar! They also make their own vodka which they liberally plied us with.

28/01/07

This morning we went on a tour to see the icebergs and wildlife. We spotted crabeater seals on a smaller low-lying iceberg, fur seals, gentoo penguins, Antarctic shags and a flock of Antarctic terns. There is an iceberg with a tunnel through it but we didn't get too close to it for fear it would calve. We also went to see an ice cave which was absolutely stunning.

Clockwise from top left: *Vernadsky base. / Wordie House Museum. / An old wooden sign claiming British Crown Land, set against a backdrop of Antarctic peaks. / A skua – one of the many around Vernadsky.*

Clockwise from top left: *JohnJohn and Ansis walk down to Wordie House. / The interior of Wordie House Museum with sleeping area and kitchen all built around a central fireplace. / Wordie House Museum, an old British base station. / Michiel outside Wordie House.*

Clockwise from top left: *A lone crabeater seal rests on an iceberg. / Crabeater seals as close up as we dare approach. / Antarctic tunnel, an iceberg with an archway through it. / Adelie penguins peer over the top of an iceberg. / Adelie penguins looking tiny on an iceberg. / A fur seal surveys his territory.*

Clockwise from top left: *Dimitri from Vernadsky base takes the crew on a dinghy ride to see some of the more spectacular icebergs around the Argentine Islands. | Icebergs come in all shapes and sizes. | Ansis talks to Vernadsky's base commander while a fur seal looks on in the background. | More icebergs!*

Climbed over ice cliff and slid down the other side to a beach where a few gentoo penguins waddled about in their cute way, wings backwards and head slightly looking up. A fur seal was lying on the stones and didn't take much notice until gulls and skuas started protesting against my presence. Then he raised his head and let out a groan. Two crabeater seals, pale beige in colour were resting on an ice shelf floating against the shore. A group of their friends darted around the piece of ice and one managed to get up on top. The view and peace of this place is delightful. There is life everywhere and breathtaking scenery of water, ice and steep high mountains and glaciers, often shrouded in several bands of cloud. Rocks of many colours, yellow, pink, black, rusty red, greenish grey, constitute the islands here, all loose eroded pieces. Unlike Mutton Cove where the rock was grey, hard, rounded stone.

Michiel's diary entry

Clockwise from top left: *The buildings of Vernadsky base station. / Denis, JohnJohn, Michael and Michiel drinking vodka in the bar at Vernadsky. / The collection of bras behind the bar. / Exchanging stamps in our passports – the boat stamp for Vernadsky's base stamp. / Two crew members walk up to the base station.*

Opposite page: *(clockwise from top left) A view out across the Argentine Islands around Vernadsky. / Dimitri holds up Vera's prized Munster scarf that she has generously given to him. /* Celtic Spirit *leaves Vernadsky.*

Ansis is invited to have dinner at the base as he is Latvian and Russian speaking. They give him surplus stocks of tinned pineapple and condensed milk for the boat. He returned with four of the people we had met the evening before including the base commander. Our resident musicians played mandolin and guitar while bottles of vodka and champagne were fed to our guests. It is a fantastic night of chat, music, singing and drinking. When they leave Vera presents her new friend Dimitri with her prized Munster scarf.

LEMAIRE CHANNEL

29/01/07

Once everyone was awake, they dealt with their hangovers and cleaned up the debris of the night before. We decided to move on to Peterman Island, a rookery for gentoo penguins. The entrance to the bay is treacherous with outlying rocks. Our two able dinghy crew went in to take a look and get depth soundings, the rest of us in the boat hung back outside the entrance. On their return they gave us the all-clear and we began making our way in. On the second attempt, we turned around and backed into the small bay. It was a very tight spot for *Celtic Spirit* and there was a lot of pressure on the dingy crew to get lines fixed ashore as we had a 20-knot wind abeam with rocks either side of us. The wind and swell made this space unnerving and lines were doubled up including a midship's line. A line was placed from shore to shore in order to prevent icebergs coming in crushing us or blocking the exit but despite this a small berg makes its way very close to us and right up against our preventative rope. The dinghy crew tried pushing the berg off with the dinghy but after a lot of useless effort we decide to get out of there in a hurry. Lines were let go and we left while the dinghy pushed our bow off. At one point the dinghy was all that separated us from the iceberg while all the time the gap was closing. We waited out in the bay until the dinghy crew had retrieved all the lines and then we headed back to Vernadsky and Stella Creek for another night. It had been an exhausting day.

30/01/07

At 1100 this morning we slipped lines and moved out from Stella Creek once more. After manoeuvring between bergy bits and icebergs

__Opposite page:__ A minke whale appears alongside the boat.
__Clockwise from right:__ Icebergs as we leave Vernadsky. / The minke whale follows us for a while. / The crew out on deck to marvel at the passing scenery of Lemaire Channel.

Clockwise from above: *We make our way through the Lemaire Channel. / We encounter sea ice, lots of it, and we have to be careful as we make our way through.*

Top (from left): *An avalanche in the Lemaire Channel.* ***Bottom (from left):*** *Another Iceberg. / We come across some traffic in the Lemaire Channel – cruise liners* Nord Norge *and* Explorer *(that sank a year later after hitting an iceberg).*

we made our way past the base and out into Penola Strait. We came across a minke whale as we continued on down past Peterman Island, where our anchorage from the evening before was now full of ice, then into Lemaire Channel (also known as Kodak Gap by the cruise liners for its photo-opportunity appeal). This is a narrow channel with steep-sided peaks on either side and absolutely breathtaking scenery. The glaciers that slope down into this strait and channel feed the waters with icebergs and bergy bits. There were a few icebergs and a large patch of sea ice that we had to make our way through. Another minke whale joined us, swimming right up against the boat, then underneath and then back again. It was stunning to have one of these creatures so close to us! A short while later ice came crashing down from the top of one of the peaks in a spectacular avalanche. We arrived into Port Lockroy and anchored off Smith Point. A great setting with mountain peaks and ice all around us in the bay.

PORT LOCKROY

31/01/07

Everyone made it over to Port Lockroy for 1000, our appointed time allowed by the base to visit. This is an old British base, now run only in the summer by three staff. It is a museum and post office where one can buy postcards, maps, t-shirts, hats and caps. It is situated in the middle of a gentoo penguin rookery and some crew found the smell of penguin poo a little overpowering to say the least. There is an increasing number of tourists making the journey to this part of Antarctica in cruise ships every year. Port Lockroy base is one of the most popular destinations and has seen an increase of 50 per cent over the previous year. While the base staff showed signs of stress, the penguins seemed unconcerned by our presence. Studies into the effects of tourism on the gentoo penguin population are being done at this base and surrounding area.

Everyone returned to the boat for lunch and later while some crew wrote postcards and diaries, others went ashore to explore. Those of us who went ashore climbed up to the top of the ridge where we walked along until we found some penguins. Walking over and down the other side of the ridge you can see across the channel. It was calm and peaceful and penguins could be seen swimming in the water. A kelp gull flew past being attacked by an Antarctic tern – such aggressive birds for their size! If you sit still for a while and watch you can see the tide carrying bits of ice down the channel. The sun made an appearance and the light cast over the landscape brought out new and interesting colours. The whole bay in which the boat was at anchor was alive with colour as the sun picked out different facets

Opposite page: *A whale skeleton at Port Lockroy with* Celtic Spirit *on the left in the distance.* | ***Right and below:*** *A gentoo penguin as he hops over rocks.* | *Port Lockroy's buildings on a rocky outcrop dwarfed by massive Antarctic peaks behind it.*

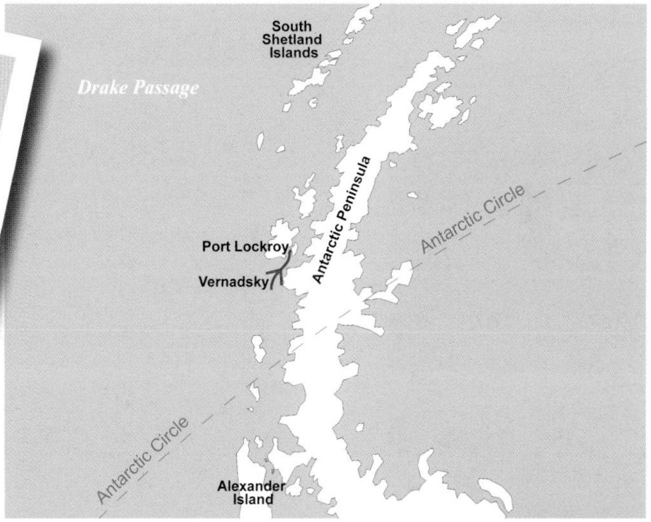

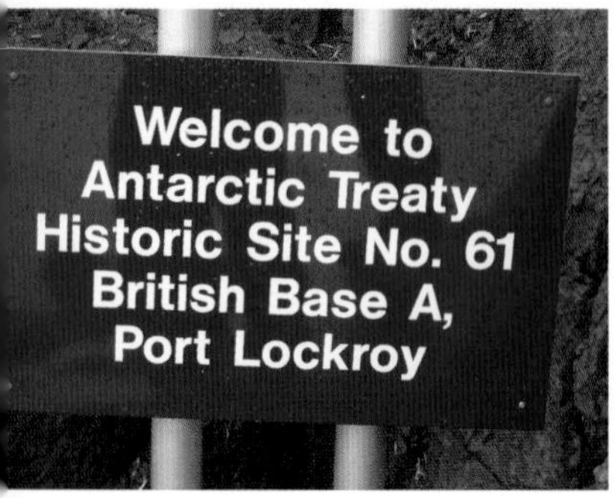

Left (from top): *Interior shots of Port Lockroy's museum and the sign outside the base building.*
Centre and above: *Port Lockroy base is mostly inhabited by gentoo penguins. / There are plenty of gentoo penguin chicks around the base at Port Lockroy, the rocks are covered in their pink brown faeces.*

of the ice. High winds were forecast and as the holding here is good, other boats were making for this protected anchorage. During the day Tony Mowbray and his boat *Commitment* had arrived and anchored not far from us. An Australian, Tony is a motivational speaker and survivor of the fateful Sydney Hobart yacht race of 1998 in which six people lost their lives during violent storm conditions. We had met him in Ushuaia and he came over for a chat. Another boat we had not encountered before, *Sadko,* also arrived to take shelter for the night, as did *Pelagic.*

I think the reason everybody loves penguins is that the television has a hard time portraying smell. If people were aware of the sensation of standing downwind of a penguin colony their popularity poll would decrease exponentially. But cute they are. Something terrible. And tiny. Like well-balanced cross breeds between infants and gala-dinner-dressed teddy bears, they waddle and shuffle around among their own faeces.

JohnJohn's diary entry

Clockwise from top left: *Gentoo penguins at the water's edge. / A gentoo in his pristine 'tux'. / Michiel's penguin drawings. / A chick eager to be fed. / A close up of a gentoo chick.*

Clockwise from above: *Janet takes a seat on a vertebra of the whale skeleton.* | *The surrounding ice landscape at Port Lockroy is streaked with red algae.* | *Whale vertebra.* | *The whale skeleton with* Celtic Spirit *in the background.* |
Centre: Celtic Spirit *and* Sadko *off Smith Point in Alice Creek.*

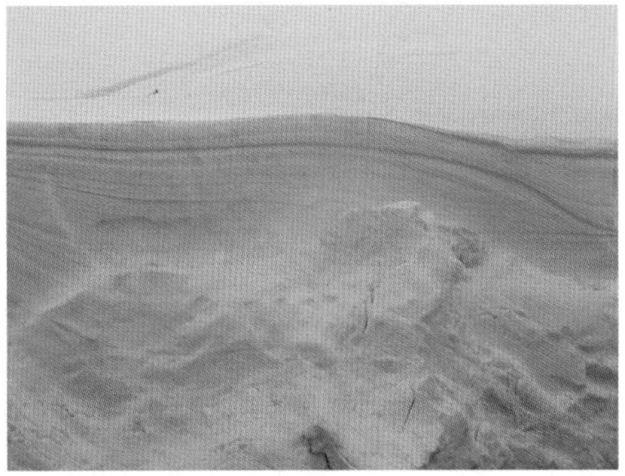

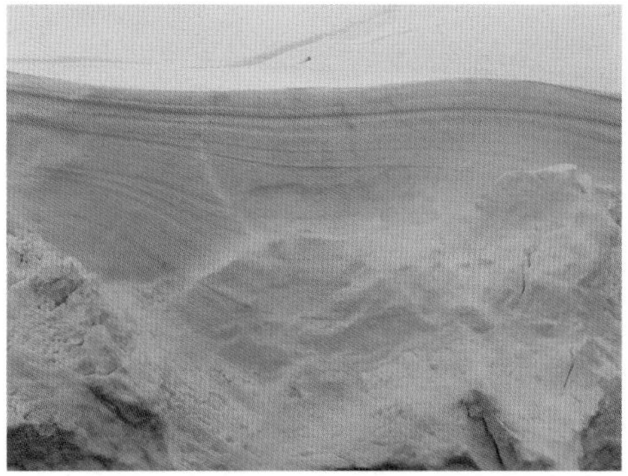

Clockwise from left: *Patterns in the ice. / The channel the other side of Port Lockroy base. / Michiel observing and drawings penguins.*

REPUBLICA ARGENTINA
BASE "MELCHIOR"
LAT 64°20' S / LONG 062°59' W
FUNDADA EL 31-03-1947

MELCHIOR BASE

01/02/07

We lifted the dinghy, weighed anchor and were off down the Neumeyer Strait and out into the Gerlache Strait once again, heading towards Melchior Island. The scenery of the peaks around us was fantastic and there was a small amount of ice but nothing too tricky. The wind was anything between 3 knots and gusting to 25. At times the sea was a little choppy which made the small pieces of ice hard to see. As we came into view, the Argentinean Melchior Base, which is situated on Gamma Island, radioed us a warm welcome, raised their flag and invited us to see their station as soon as we were ready. We made our way into the little cove as soon as the dinghy crew was satisfied that it was safe to do so. There was wind gusting over 20 knots but inside the cove it was calmer. However, there was a significant swell and space was tight. Lines were tied on quickly and then doubled. One of the stern lines snapped with the strain of the swell and there was frantic activity to get the lines even and secure again for the night. Not everyone slept well during the night due to the creaking of lines and the uncomfortable swell.

02/02/07

The skipper was unhappy with our position and wanted to turn the boat around so that we could get out in a hurry if we needed to. The

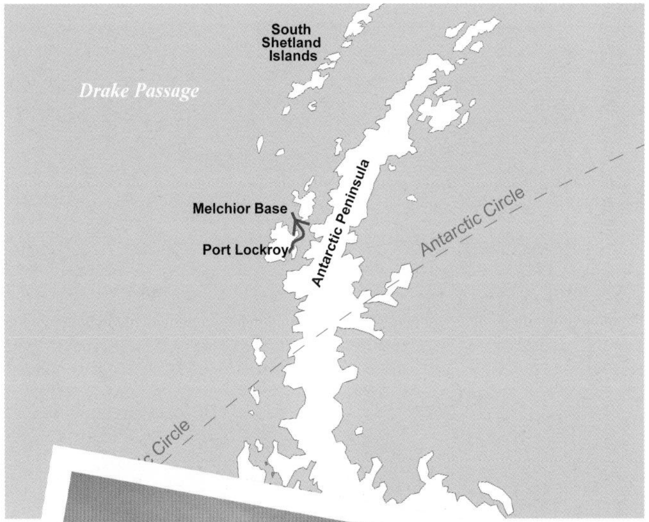

'... the good news is that I now know EXACTLY how long it takes for my hands to thaw enough to feel pain again.' After beating a hasty retreat from the narrow anchorage at Melchior station, dropping all the lines in the water and barehanded untangling and collecting the mess.

JohnJohn's diary entry

Opposite page: *Ansis and Denis chat with the commander of Melchior Base as they fill a container with fuel outside the base buildings.* /
Right and far right: *Melchior Base comes into view.* / *The base station buildings as seen from the cove where we tie up – note the steel pitons in the rock in the foreground.*

Clockwise from far left: *Our skipper with Martin, the base commander and Frederico, the head architect. / Melchior Base. / The crew sit around the table wearing their Melchior Base caps. / The crew and base staff gather for a group shot. / Blayney tucking into empanadas and Argentinian wine. / Michiel and JohnJohn with the Argentinian flag behind them.*

wind and the swell seemed to be increasing. While we were still trying to make a decision as to where to go, the Argentineans invited us for dinner. Another line snapped and so we decided it was best to reverse out and anchor in the bay. By now, it was snowing.

Just before 2200 we made our way over to the base in two dinghy loads. This base is staffed by Navy personnel who are carrying out modifications to the base and who will remain there for four months. They have no communication with the outside world except directly to their command centre in Buenos Aires. They do not have even a small boat and are prohibited from leaving the base. Because of its location, very few boats visit this area. Martin, the base commander, was very welcoming and asked us to sign the visitors' book and offered us brochures on Argentina. They had envelopes and stamps as well as badges and caps for sale. Martin gave a short speech on the base and then brought us through to the dining room. This was typical Argentinean fare: cheese, ham and olives for starters and empanadas (described by a crew member as Cornish pasties) for the main course. It was all washed down with copious amounts of red and white wine. We had a great time chatting to them. We were given a present of two bottles of Argentinean wine, one red and one white, on our departure, one of which we drank once back aboard the boat later.

Clockwise from top left: *A weddel seal, fur seal and* Celtic Spirit *at anchor in the background.* | *Our skipper and the base commander walking down the stairs from Melchior Base.* | *Melchior Base on its rocky island.* | *Fur seals.* | *A sleepy weddel seal.*

Melchior Islands ahead to starboard. Just finished two-hour watch. Freezing wind, cold toes in spite of Canadian boots. Fantastic sky with bits of sun shafts and all colours of clouds on the high mountains covered with sun, ice and glaciers. Melchior looks like a desolate spot. Humpback whales breaching, spouting. Arrived at Gamma Island south shore, making a wide berth around shoals of Normanna reef between Omega and Gamma Islands. Followed south-east shore as far as orange Argentinean huts. Base called on channel 16 and displayed a big welcome including raising their beloved flag. Dropped dinghy outside gallows point in 25 to 30 knots of south-easterly wind in order to prepare tie on points. Creek faces northeast so is sheltered but a lot of lines were needed to secure our 50-ton ship. Dynema starboard stern line tore and steel wire snapped. Wind calmed in mooring but big swell. Had to back out in a hurry as starboard line broke with the swell. Dropped lines and moved to anchor in bay northwest of base.

Michiel's diary entry

ANDERSON HARBOUR

03/02/07

Everyone was slow to rise after our late night at Melchior Base. It took some time to get organised and after going over to the base to drop off the postcards and saying goodbye, we weighed anchor and moved over to Anderson Harbour across the bay between Eta and Omega Islands where it took some time to find a suitable spot to anchor. Depths were tricky and the charts and GPS positions did not match. This meant navigating using landmarks and bearings. After a lunch of soup and toast it was time for exploring. We went into the narrow channel between the islands to explore depths and some crew members landed ashore and then climbed up the rocky side of the cliff, leaving the skipper on the boat on anchor watch. Parts of the cliff face were very loose and dangerous, however, once we reached the top the view was superb. While on our travels we discovered a rusty old spade, piping and an old sailor's hat, possibly a military one. A yacht we had previously seen arrived into the channel and anchored in the shelter of the little cove. We took the dinghy over to the next beach where Ansis had a good vantage point to photograph *Celtic Spirit*. Janet watched a large adult seal swim with his head above the water right at the water's edge. He got closer and closer, and then came up onto the beach right next to where she was sitting. The seal waddled all the way past and up onto the ice where he made himself a cosy bed and went for a snooze. As holding was very poor a second anchor was dropped and an anchor watch was set up for the night.

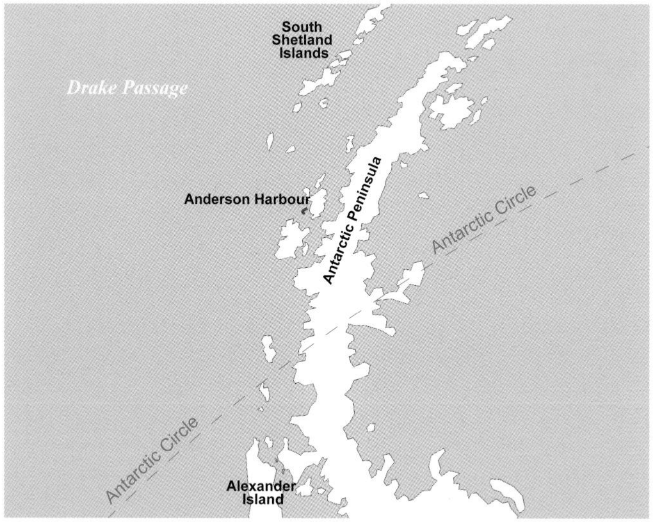

Opposite page: *Entering Anderson Harbour, beautiful calm and quiet.* / ***Left and above:*** *Rocky mounds covered in ice.* / *Crevasses in the ice reflect a bright blue.*

Clockwise from bottom left: *Peace and calm around Anderson Harbour.* | Celtic Spirit *at anchor in Anderson Harbour.* | *Ansis doing his best to look like a professional photographer.*

Opposite page: *(left top to bottom) A Weddel seal makes its way up the beach.* | *(centre top and bottom) Ice bergs drift past.* | *Our boat snowman keeps watch at the helm.* | *(right) The moonlight over Anderson Harbour.*

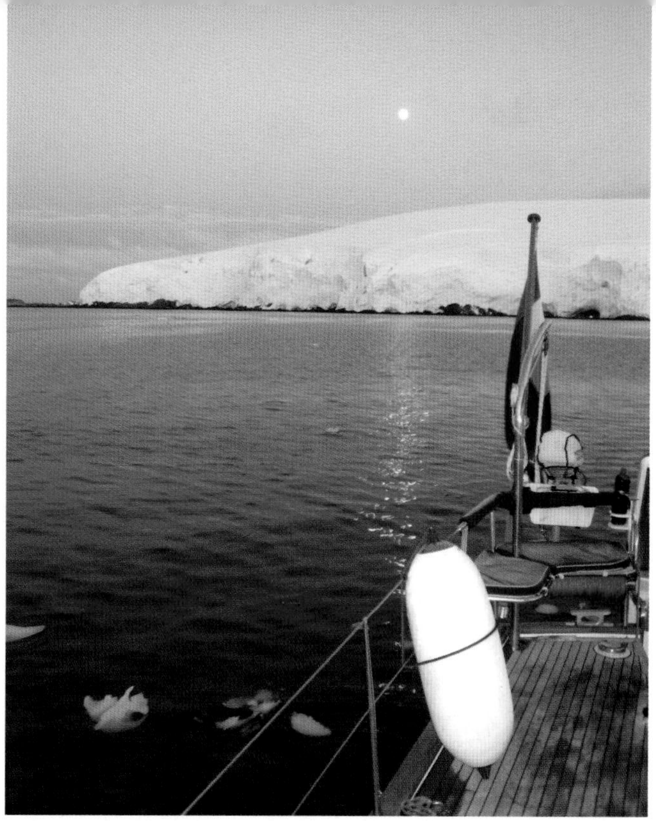

Got up at 0500 this morning for anchor watch here in Anderson Harbour. We are in 18 m water and have two anchors out but neither are well dug in because of the stony bottom. There is little to no wind so no problem there but I have to watch a big iceberg that is drifting slowly this way into the bay. I've switched on the radar to monitor its distance to the ship. The sun just came up over the edge of the ice-capped land to the east. It is a beautiful tranquil scene. Terns and skuas are the only moving things and all is quiet on board too.

Michiel's diary entry

CUVERVILLE ISLAND

04/02/07

During last night a lot of ice came into the bay including a large berg that had to be watched. Thankfully, it was blown past us and eventually grounded. We set sail early and as we passed Melchior Base we radioed our new Navy friends. However, it was a Sunday and they must have been having a sleep-in as we got no response. We made our way out into the Gerlache Strait. In the strait we encountered a pod of humpback whales. It seemed as if we were converging on the same course so we slowed and they moved behind, alongside and ahead of us. It was fantastic to watch them. We motored across the strait and over to Cuverville Island and dropped anchor. This is a wonderful spot where the gentoo penguins are friendly and the view is unbelievably stunning. There are bergs in the bay and the sun came out, casting a fantastic afternoon light over everything. The penguins were interesting to watch as they fed their young.

As soon as all crew were back onboard we weighed anchor, headed back out into the strait and travelled northeast up to Enterprise Island. The surrounding mountains and scenery on the way was spectacular once again. As we neared Enterprise Island we slowed in order to launch the dinghy. There were bergs and it was unclear as to the depth in the channel ahead. Our dinghy

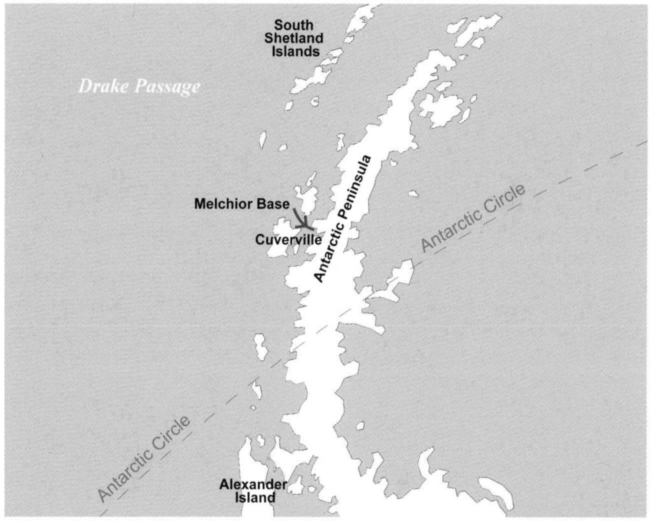

Opposite page: Celtic Spirit *against the landscape of peaks in Cuverville.* | ***Clockwise from above:*** *Humpback whales in the Gerlache Strait.* | *Penguins in the foreground with* Celtic Spirit *at anchor in the background.*

Clockwise from right: *Penguins and icebergs. / A whale vertebra on the rocky beach in Cuverville. / Two penguin chicks wait patiently to be fed. / An adult gentoo penguin.*

Left and above: *Penguins as far as the eye can see.* /
Bottom: *(from left) A penguin rushes to feed its young.* / *Penguin art!*

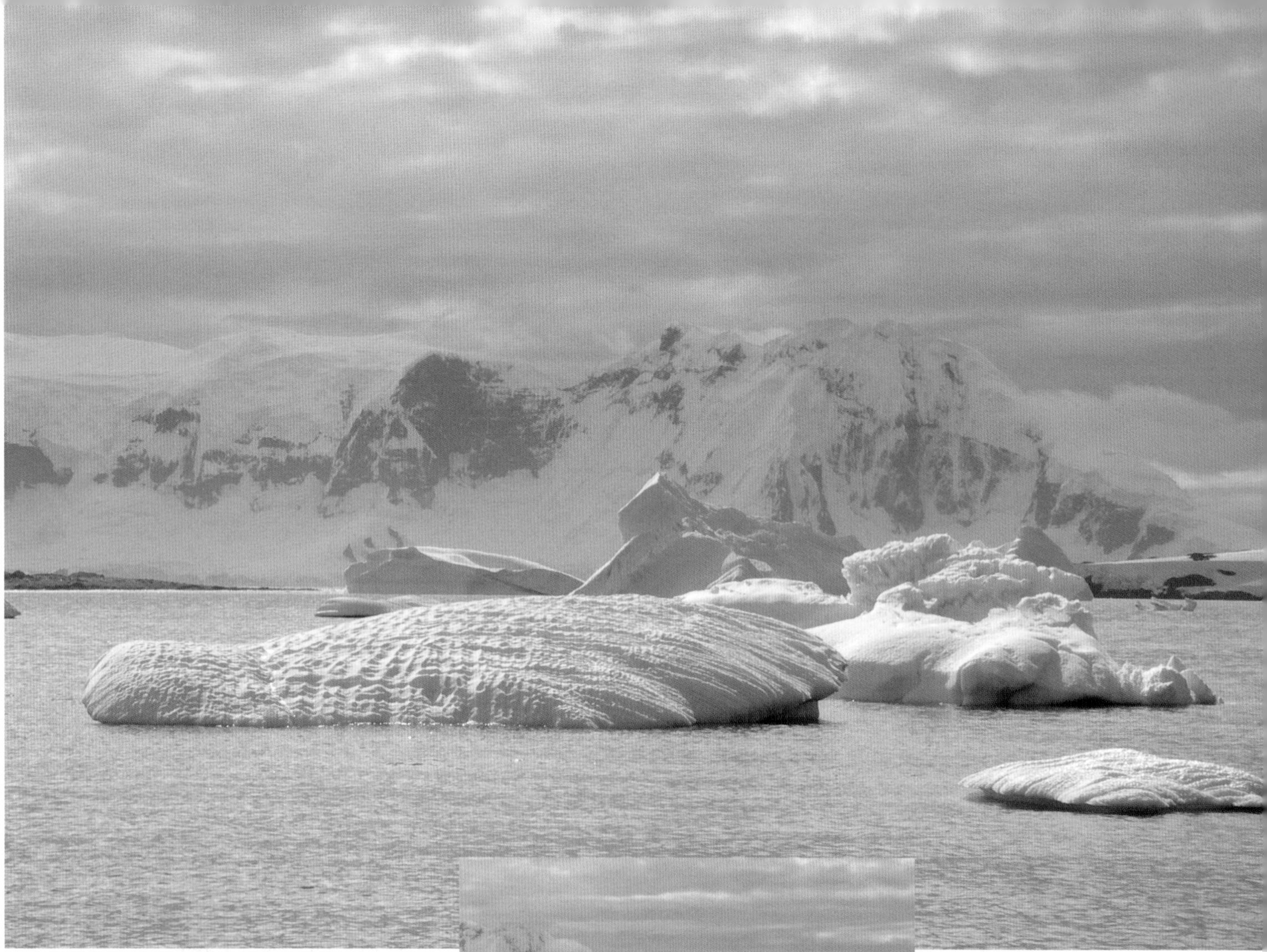

Clockwise from bottom left:
Snow-capped peaks surround the bay in Cuverville. | Icebergs of all shapes and sizes litter the bay. | A piece of ice on the water's edge. | Small pieces of ice amongst the stones on the beach.

crew reported that it was very shallow in places so we entered the anchorage from a different aspect. We moved forward slowly, with the dinghy going ahead to check depths, and finally made our way in next to the wreck of a ship where *Pelagic* was tied up on the other side. Just after the wreck it shallows very quickly. It was around 2200 by the time we came in and tied up. Dinner was served as soon as everyone was ready and was consumed enthusiastically. Afterwards, punch was made with leftovers from the bar and a large piece of Antarctic ice was found and added to the 'punch bowl'.

Clockwise from top left : *Spectacular Antarctic peaks. / Ice scattered below the peaks. / Penguins, icebergs,* Celtic Spirit *and the mountain peaks of Antarctica. / More icebergs across the bay.*

ENTERPRISE ISLAND

05/02/07

The crew began surfacing around mid-morning. It had snowed heavily during the night and the boat was covered in a thick layer. The water around the boat and into the cove had begun to ice up. *Northern Light*, a well known Swedish yacht we had encountered on our arrival in Ushuaia, appeared through the mist and snow. We invited them to tie up alongside us. They did not stay long as they felt the winds were now good for them to travel further south. Their intention was to overwinter in Antarctica as they had done before. *Northern Light* is owned and sailed by Rolf Bjelke and Deborah Shapiro who have written several books on their experiences in Antarctica. Our skipper decided that it was an opportune time to fix the heating, which had not been working and so the afternoon was spent doing this.

Opposite page: Celtic Spirit *next to the shipwreck at Enterprise Island.* | **Left above and right:** *Snow covers the winches after a night of heavy snowfall.* | *Our dinghy gets a dose of snow.* | *The surrounding water begins to ice up.*

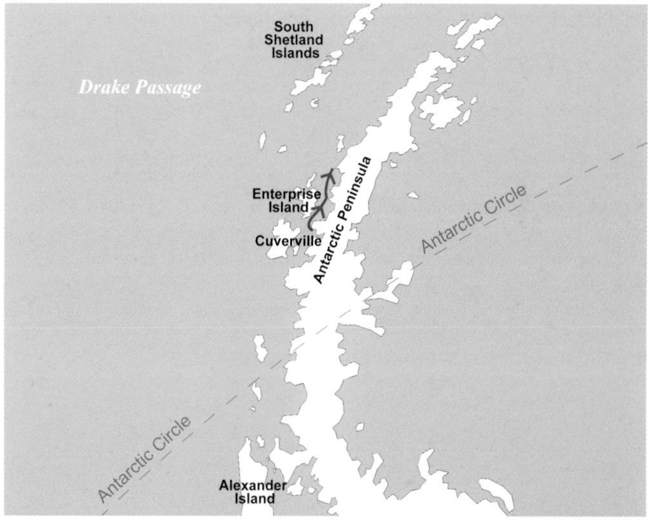

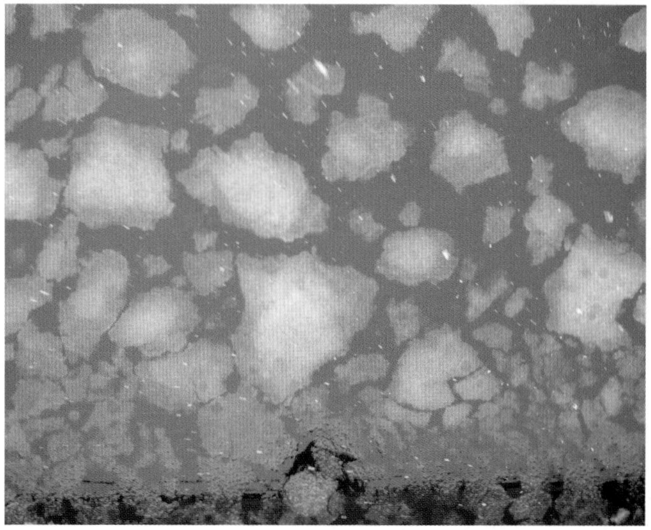

5th February 2007
A big sincere thank you to all my crew mates on Celtic Spirit for a fabulous birthday celebration over dinner and beyond last night. A great dinner, fresh apple tart dessert and a specially concealed bottle of gin/tonic to complement the proceedings. A wonderful card signed by all and a special present of 'frosties' cereal completed the occasion. I very much appreciated everything and had a great evening. Again, my sincere thanks to all.

Blayney

Clockwise from above: Celtic Spirit *tied up to the shipwreck at Enterprise Island.* | *Blayney with his birthday presents.* | *Blayney's birthday pies.* | Northern Light *departs.*

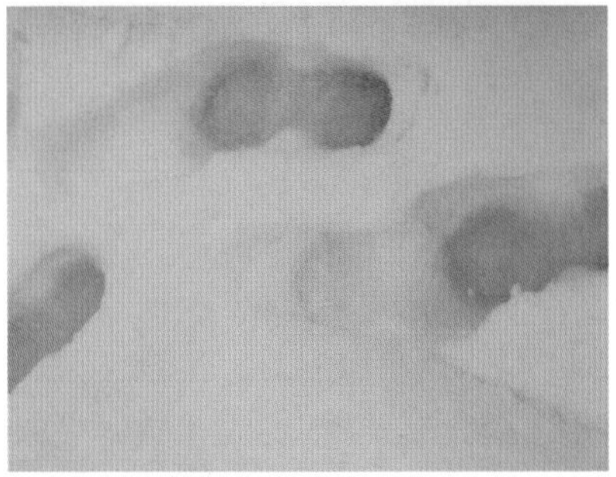

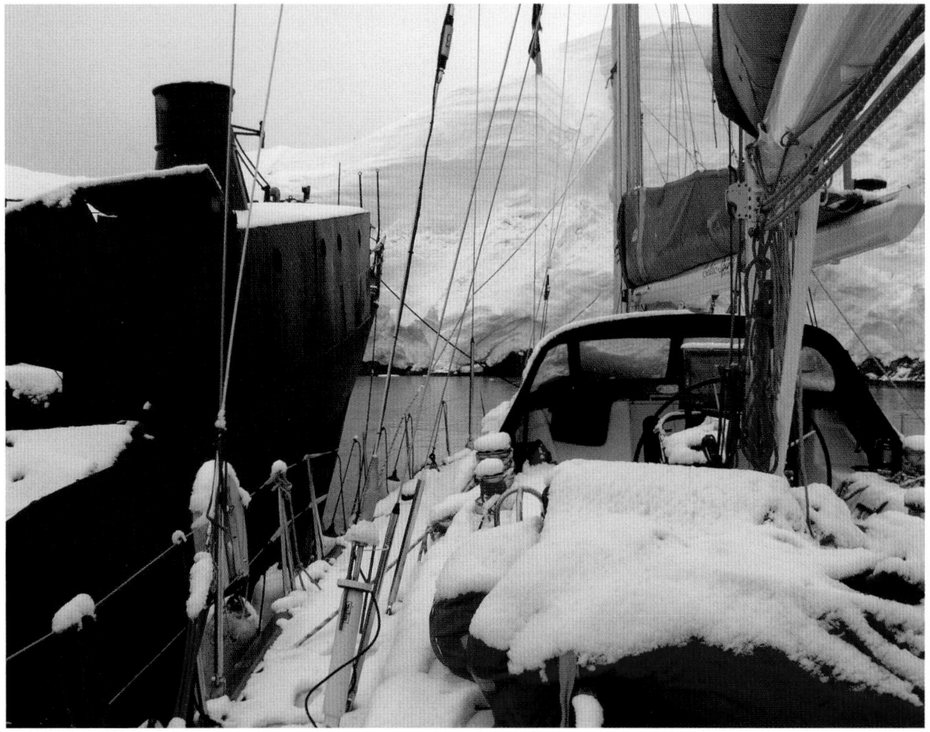

Clockwise from top left: Celtic Spirit *by night tied up to the rusty wreck.* / *JohnJohn learns to play Michiel's mandolin.* / *Our punch bowl – complete with Antarctic ice.* / Celtic Spirit *covered in snow.* / *Footprints in the snow.*

However, it stubbornly refused to function so we were to continue as before, living in a fridge! We had a brief visit from Gisele, a South-African crew member from *Pelagic* who brought over some apples and oranges. We celebrated Blayney's birthday with the last bottle of gin and tonic at dinner. Michiel had custom made a 'birthday cake' in the form of two apple pies (with the aid of an egg 'borrowed' from *Northern Light*) and we ate it with the condensed milk donated by Vernadsky, followed by more punch.

06/02/07

Again this morning there was snow on the decks although nowhere near as much as yesterday. There seemed to be more ice around. A dinghy ride took us over across the bay to where numerous fur seals were reclining on the rocks. There was a swell and so many seals that we could not land and so we went over to the wrecks of three abandoned whaling boats instead. Here we found some more seals perched on nearby rocks. On our way back we passed close to a seal and a beautiful iceberg with the most incredible jagged shape. On arrival back at the boat we let the rest of the crew go out exploring and looking for water. This we got from ice that was melting a short

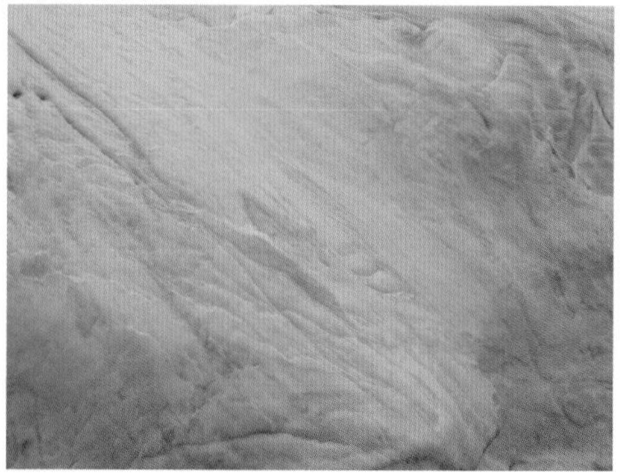

Clockwise from above: *Details of the rusty shipwrecked whale boat.* / Celtic Spirit *tied up to the left of the wreck and* Pelagic *to the right.* / *Ice surrounding us.*

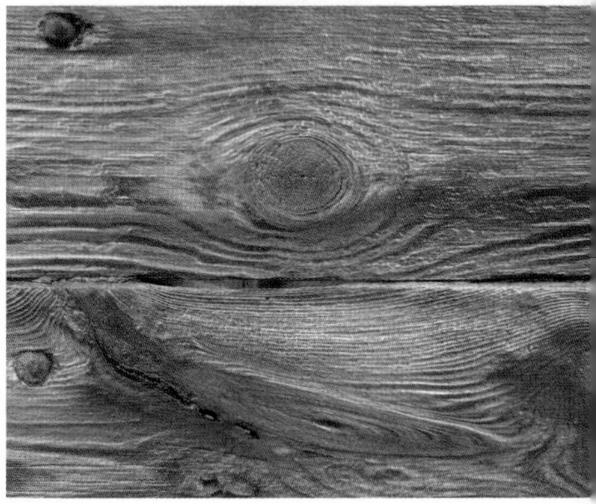

Clockwise from above: *Old wooden whaling boats abandoned on a rocky outcrop not far from the wreck where we are tied up. / Details of the whaling boats.*

Clockwise from top left: *Fur seals on the rocks. / Ansis, Blayney and JohnJohn walking on a floating piece of ice. / Icebergs near Enterprise Island. / A photo shoot on an iceberg.*

distance from the boat. The dinghy was filled with this water and then it was pumped from there into our tanks. It was decided to head for Challenger Island. We had dinner just before we arrived and then made our way into the bay and dropped anchor. It took ages to find the right spot and even then the anchor seemed to be dragging slightly. The bottom was all rock so holding was poor and our normal watch system was continued instead of a separate anchor watch. This would make it easier to depart for Deception Island as soon as it was daylight.

Clockwise from bottom left: *The passing ice-scapes as we leave Enterprise Island.* / *Terns fly overhead.* / *The last sight of mainland Antarctica as we head for Deception Island.*

DECEPTION ISLAND

07/02/07

Having left Murray Bay and Challenger Island very early we made good time to Deception Island 90 miles away in winds of 10 to 20 knots from the southwest. The day was back to normal watches and we saw the occasional humpback whale and very little ice. It was beautiful and sunny and for the first time since our crossing of the Drake Passage, we had albatrosses flying with us again. We arrived into Neptune's Bellows, the entrance to Deception Island, around 1800 and made our way over to Telefon Bay where we took a long time to anchor in soft mud using 80 m of heavy chain and our Bruce anchor. Deception Island is an old sunken volcanic crater, which is dormant but not dead. The landscape is bare sand and is really quite bleak looking. Across from us on a little beach we can see some fur seals.

08/02/07

Making an early start, four of the crew got ready and went over to the shore. They walked up onto the ridge and found a sign from Greenpeace warning that it was an area of scientific importance so they decided to walk in the other direction to the very top of the crater and over to the other side. The terrain was tricky in places because erosion had caused a lot of cracks and crevices. There were interesting mounds of yellow stone that had shattered presumably as they had been pushed up and reached the surface. From the very top they could see humpback whales out in the ocean as well as Livingston Island. Then they scrambled back down the hill and they walked along the water's edge to the next cove where they found a lone, elderly gentoo

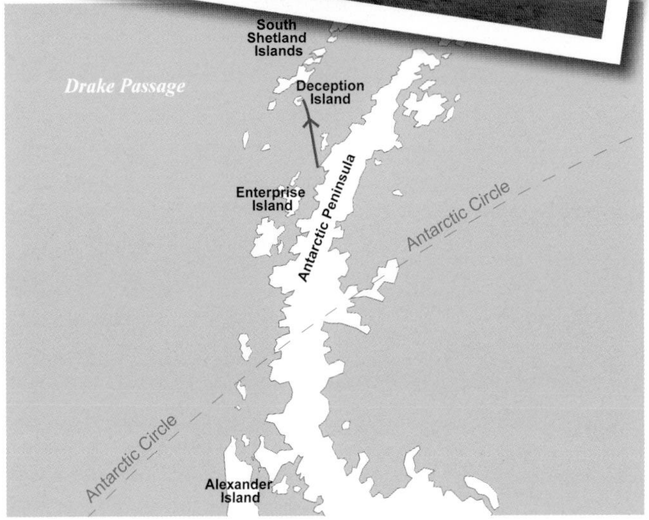

Opposite page: *View across the inside of the crater of Deception Island.* ***Clockwise from top left:*** *The entrance to Deception Island, Neptune's Bellows. / Rocky cliffs to the right of the entrance. / Cape petrels at the cliffs of Neptune's Bellows.*

penguin. After lunch we moved the boat to Pendulum Cove where the water is warm in places due to the volcanic activity. It is, in fact, the ground that is hot – in some places scalding hot. The water is freezing. Most of the crew had a 'swim'; in most cases this was a quick wetting although others stayed in for a while. Then it was over to the shore for some exploring through the ruins of a Chilean base that had been destroyed by volcanic activity in 1967. After this we moved the boat back to Telefon Bay as the holding was better there and it was more protected. As soon as the anchor was down we had dinner, washed down with some wine. After this there was a mass clean-up and everything on deck and below deck was stowed in preparation for the Drake Passage the next day.

Clockwise from top left: *Michiel and the Greenpeace sign. / The landscape of Deception Island – snow-capped mountains of dark sand. / Eroded volcanic sand dunes. / The view from the top of the volcanic crater, Livingston Island in the distance.*

Clockwise from top left: Celtic Spirit *anchored in Telefon Bay set against the multi-coloured volcanic sand mountains.* / *The centre of Deception Island and the entrance to Telefon Bay.* / Celtic Spirit *looking small in the vast expanse of Telefon Bay.* / *Ochre coloured rocks stand out against the dark brown sands of Deception Island.*

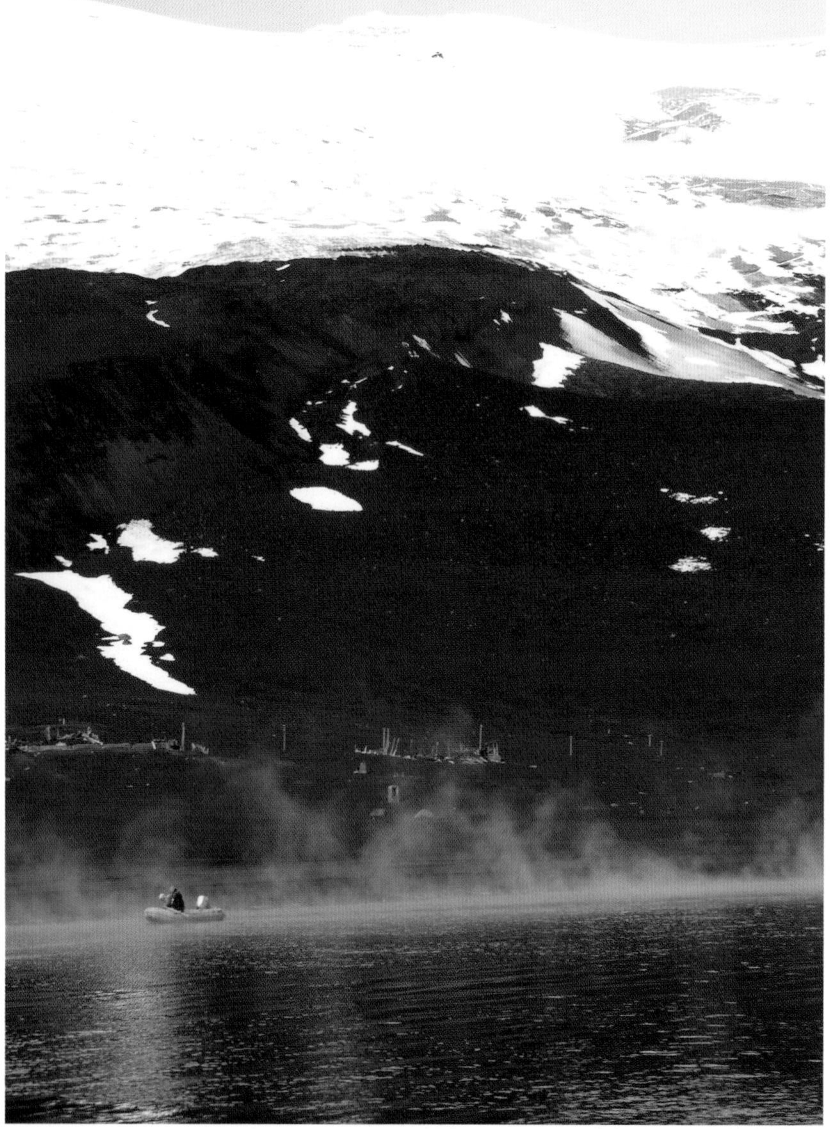

Clockwise from top left: Celtic Spirit *leaves Telefon Bay for Pendulum Cove. / The dinghy amongst the steam at the water's edge; the ruins of the Chilean base remain at the foot of the crater with its snow-capped peaks behind. / Pendulum Cove. / A lone chinstrap penguin with Pendulum Cove in the background.*

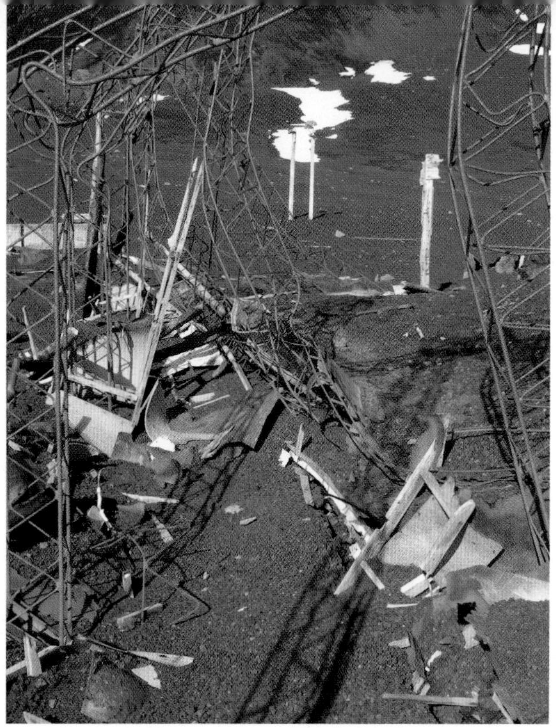

Climbed ridge of Deception with JohnJohn and tried to walk along to Pendulum Cove then drop down and swim in hot water. Realised three quarters of the way there that we were actually on a glacier. Deep crevasses under volcanic matter. Scary. Back tracked. Scrambled down some of the way and then walked over undulating ash. Like a moon-scape. View from above stunning. One side crater, the other side Livingston, snow, low islands. Whales jumping in calm sea.

Michiel's diary entry

Clockwise from above: *The remains of the Chilean base destroyed in 1967. / The black landscape at Pendulum Cove.*

DRAKE PASSAGE

09/02/07

Celtic Spirit left Telefon Bay around 0400 in order to get an early start. We weigh anchor and head into a beautiful sunrise and out of Deception Island with winds between 15 to 20 knots. Outside, the sea is lumpy and, until we can get the sails up, it is like being inside a washing machine. We sail with reefed main and genoa in winds between 27 to 37 knots from the southwest. It was cold and overcast. Black-browed albatross and Cape petrels were flying with us. We manually helm the boat and half an hour is enough to have

Clockwise from left: *Ansis gets ready to go snow boarding. / Red and black sand mix with snow and ice on the slopes of the crater at Pendulum Cove. / Layers of ice and ash create patterns and a hazard if you attempt to walk over what looks like solid ground.*

Got up at four o'clock this morning to lift anchor from Telefon Bay in Deception Island. Sky strange spaceship clouds at sunrise, pink orange. Fog on high ground of the volcano. Neptune's Bellows still calm, Cape petrels at cliff. Ready to 'dash' across the Drake. Bit scarred as NNW strong winds (50 knots) expected Sunday. Matter of speed. Today 25–30 knots SW expected.

Michiel's diary entry

your hands and feet frozen. Everyone took to their beds when not on watch. It's the only warm place on board.

10/02/07

The wind slackened off during the night and moved around to the north. At one point it was below 20 knots and we had the engines on. Everyone was eating so this is a good sign that they are managing to ward off sickness. Making soup and toast was a challenge as the cooker swung wildly, spilling soup and the toaster needed minding so as not to let it smash into the microwave door. Co-ordinating warm toast and bowls of soup was not easy.

11/02/07

Today the winds are around 20 knots and dying. We bring out more genny and shake out a reef in the main. Eventually the wind is down to 13 knots and it moves around to the north so we are forced to motor sail. It is slowly getting warmer. Water temperature has risen, to plus 1.6 °C and so has the air temperature. A whale is spotted. The forecast is to be the same for the next day. It also starts to drizzle.

12/02/07

We are now nearing the Beagle Canal and have almost made it across the infamous Drake Passage. A few cruise liners are spotted and the albatrosses and petrels are still flying with us. The coastline becomes increasingly clearer as the day goes on and we can smell land. The water temperature has risen to 5.6 °C. We all enjoy the trip into the Beagle Canal and around 2030 we arrive into Bahia Relegada where we anchor in soft mud and have dinner. We will stay here for the night and go exploring this beautiful bay tomorrow.

Clockwise from above: Celtic Spirit *makes her way across the waters of Deception Island to Neptune's Bellows as the sun comes up.* / *View from the entrance to Telefon Bay across to Pendulum Cove.* / Celtic Spirit *is under sail as we approach the Beagle Canal.*

BEAGLE CANAL

13/02/07

This morning brings the most beautiful sunrise. The air is so still that the mountains are mirrored in the water. Half the crew get up early and go over to the shore for a walk. The area is so peaceful and quiet that sound carries from the boat clearly to the shore. We walk along the water's edge for some way then head up onto the road and back toward the Estancia Harberton which is one of the oldest ranches in Tierra del Fuego. It is 22,000 hectares and it is still managed by the descendants of the original owners, the Bridges family. On the way we see a fox as he patrols the paths he has worn in the grass. The first building we come to inside the Estancia grounds is a museum, Acatushun. We go inside and are given an interesting and well-presented guided tour by Andrea, a volunteer and biology student working there. Most of the exhibits are skeletons of mammals that died from beach strandings. These include all types of dolphins and whales, and one of the rarest skeletons of a beaked whale. We go behind the scenes and see how the curators catalogue the bones and also visit the boil house where they boil all the flesh from the bones and clean them before assembly. Then we continue on to the Estancia. There is a restaurant up on the hill with a fantastic view and we have lunch here. It pours rain so we stay and have a coffee. Once the rain has stopped we venture on and find the coffee shop where we hope to ask if they will have us for dinner. The owner agrees and says they will make us dinner for 1930. After our simple but delicious dinner we retire back to the boat where our resident musicians treat us to a night of music and song.

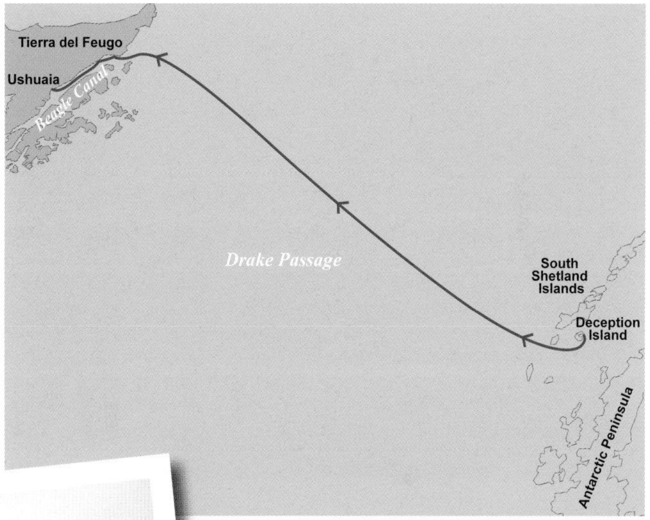

Opposite page: *Cattle roam the grounds of Estancia Remolinos.* / ***Clockwise from above:*** Celtic Spirit *at anchor in the Beagle.* / *Calm waters and mountain peaks surround us.*

Clockwise from bottom left: *The grounds of Estancia Harbeton. / Museum Acatushun. / The boil house. / Bones are stored ready for cataloguing. / A carcass ready for boiling. / A volunteer at work in the boil house.*

The calmest sunrise and again the sense of smells and birdsong as if I hadn't heard it for years. How lucky to live where there is green and relative warmth. The place to see orcas show their young how to beach to catch sea lions is the Peninsula Valdez in November.

All this and more info at the museum of sea mammals and birds and their numerous skeletons situated at the Harberton Estancia. This place is a time-warp collection of corrugated houses and sheds including workshop, boathouse, stables and big house. There is a jetty and tea house that serves English style cakes. Denis and Vera treated all to a delicious wholesome meal including rhubarb crumble. This was after a super walk with JohnJohn into the hills and along a river. It all is such a contrast to Antarctica, the scare of the Drake, the cold, cold sea; as much as I am amazed, enchanted and surprised and I would love to return to climb the ice, it feels like coming home even though Tierra del Fuego can't be much further from my home place ... or has this become home too?

Michiel's diary entry

Left: *Ansis, Michael and Blayney walk down the road to Estancia Harberton.* | ***Below:*** *Michiel's drawing of an old truck parked next to the corrugated sheds behind the wooden fences on the estancia.*

14/02/07

Today we leave to move further down the Beagle to Estancia Remolinas, which is the second oldest Estancia in Tierra del Fuego. This is past Isla Gable and Puerto Williams. We eat the last pizza and loaf of bread for lunch with the last slices of ham. The wind is around 14 knots from the southeast so we are able to get some sail up for a while. At 1700 we arrive and drop anchor. The dinner watch decides that we should have a barbeque onshore so we go over to find a suitable spot and collect firewood. Preparations are made onboard and then we hit the shore where the fire is ablaze. Dinner is barbequed burgers, chicken and steak accompanied by chilli and chicken pasta. It is delicious and we finished it off with the last of our wine supply. The estancia itself is run down and has not been looked after. There is a graveyard up on the hill where the original founders, the Lawrence family, are buried. They inherited the estate from the government for their benevolent works for the local Indian inhabitants. The sunset is breathtaking and includes a spectacular rainbow. Michiel

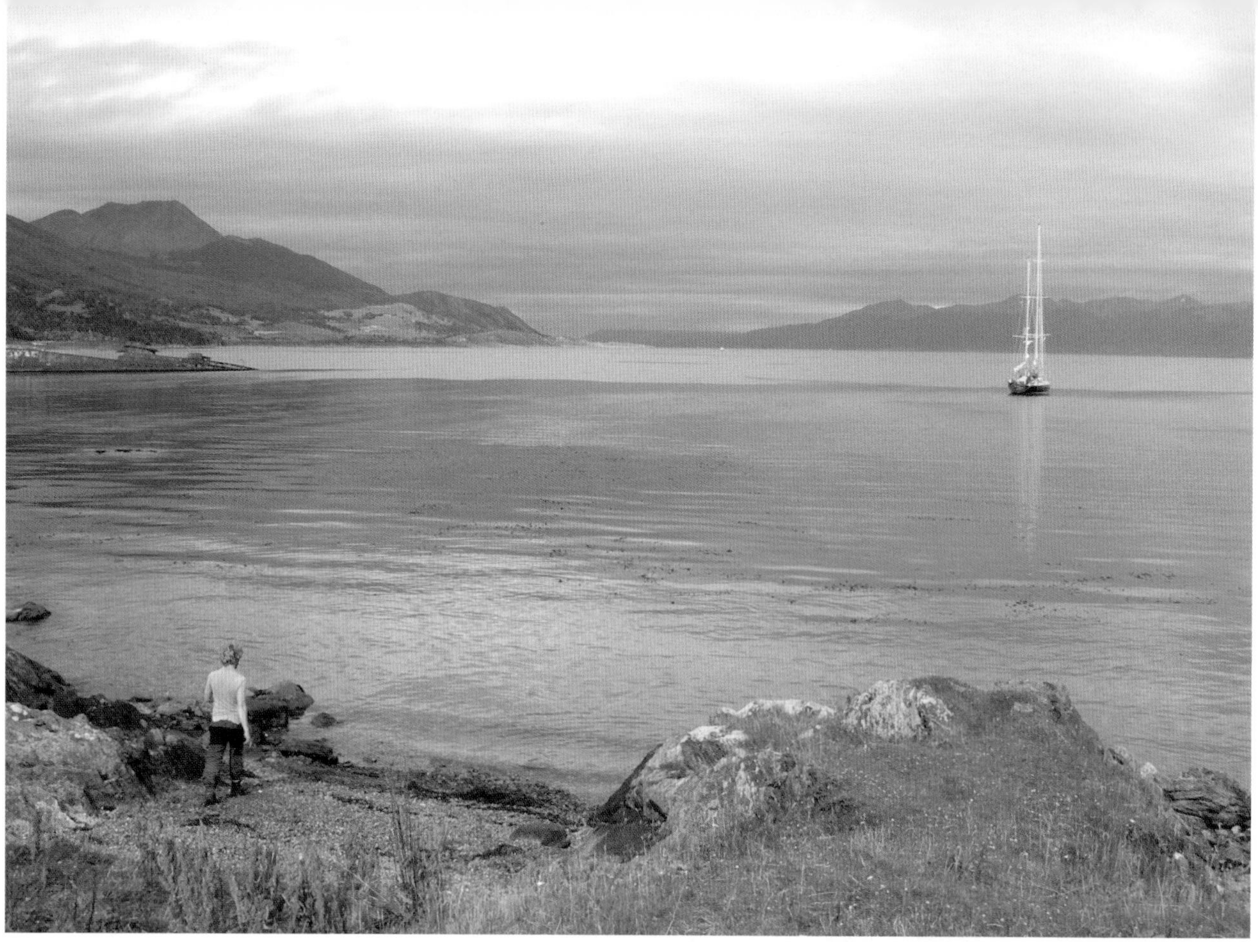

Opposite page (clockwise from top right): *JohnJohn at the water's edge with* Celtic Spirit *at anchor.* | *The crew choose a spot for the evening barbeque.* | *Buildings, the pier and shipwreck at Estancia Remolinos.*

Clockwise from left: Celtic Spirit *at anchor in the Beagle Canal.* | *JohnJohn and Michiel prepare the food for the barbeque.* | *The crew tucks into their dinner.* | *JohnJohn, Michael, Janet, Ansis (and umbrella), Blayney, Denis, Vera and Michiel with* Celtic Spirit *in the background.* | *Our fire.* | *Ansis, Denis, Vera and Blayney wait patiently for their dinner.*

Clockwise from right: *Calafatte berries. / The road out of Estancia Remolino. / A rainbow over the Beagle Canal. / The hills of Estancia Remolino.*
Opposite page: *(top) Michiel's drawing of* Celtic Spirit *at anchor at Estancia Remolino. / (bottom from left) An old wreck lies in the waters of the Beagle Canal. / An old wooden walkway. / The sun sets on the Beagle Canal.*

and JohnJohn decide to walk to Ushuaia the following day and sleep ashore by the fire so that they can make an early start. It is a 22-mile walk along the coastline!

15/02/07

This morning we collected the sleeping bags left behind by Michiel and JohnJohn who departed 0500 on their long hike to Ushuaia and around 1100 we weigh anchor and depart down the Beagle. *Celtic Spirit* arrives in Ushuaia around 1500 and we anchor in the bay to await the tide and a suitable spot to berth, finally moving alongside the pontoon around 2030. This is where *Celtic Spirit* will remain for about six days and provision with supplies for more than a month before continuing on to South Georgia, Tristan da Cunha and finally South Africa. It is nearly one month since *Celtic Spirit* departed from Ushuaia for Antarctica and the return here represents the penultimate challenge to our voyage.

Puerto Williams and the Southern Ocean

Leaving Ushuaia, Argentina for the last time, we make our way down the Beagle Canal visiting Puerto Williams on its Chilean side briefly before heading out into the infamous Southern Ocean en route to South Georgia.

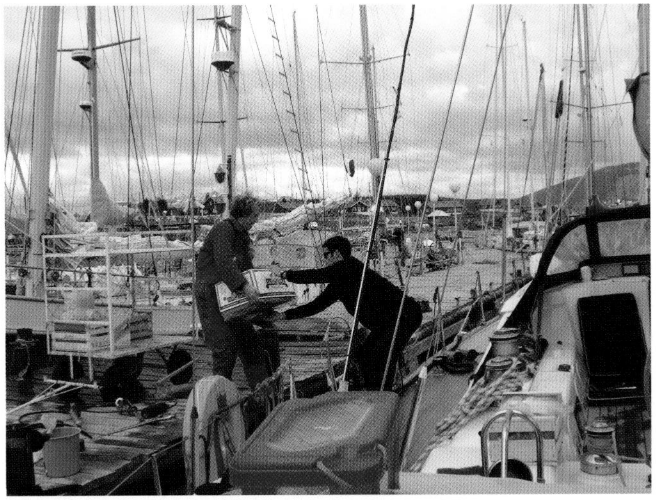

Opposite page: *The wide expanse of the Beagle Canal, which separates Argentina and Chile, lined on either side by hills and mountains.* | **Above and right:** *Michiel and Fabrizio load boxes of food on board.* | *Fabrizio wraps loaves of bread in cling film to keep them as fresh as possible.*

24/02/07

After a hectic day of sorting out the last provisioning, tidying up the boat and saying our goodbyes to Ushuaia and our friends there, we slipped our lines and were off down the Beagle Canal. It took us four hours to get to Puerto Williams, Chile where we dropped anchor. Our plan was to visit and land on Cape Horn, which belongs to Chile. After a quick dinner, the skipper completed the formalities of checking in and once we are cleared in, all the crew head over to the pub, which is in a wreck of an old ship that lists at an angle. It has a wood-burning stove in the corner that keeps the cabin warm. Here we meet Denis and Vera who have come over on the ferry for a visit. The walls

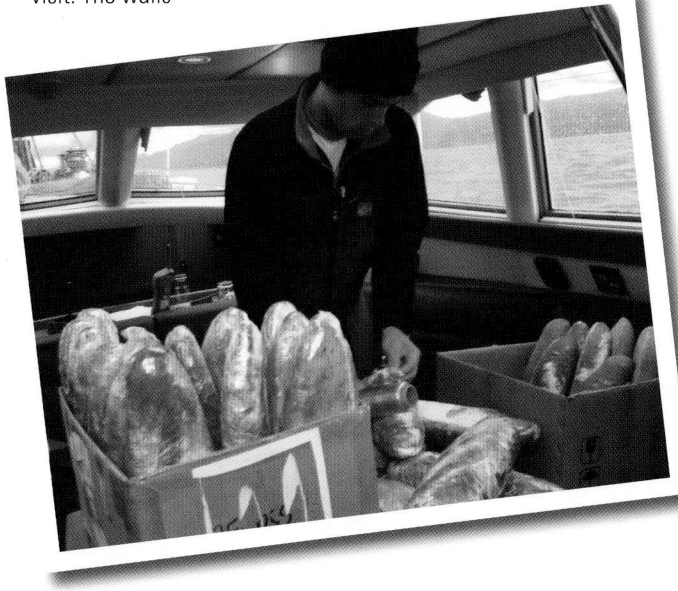

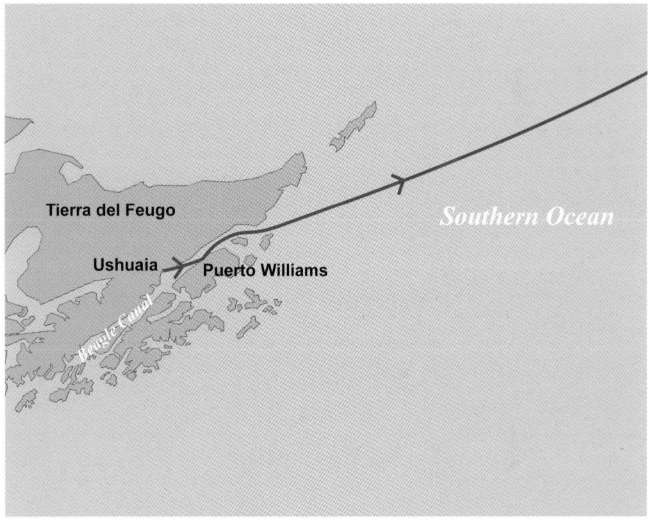

are covered in pendants and flags from boats that have visited here over the years. We brought our own flag, signed it and staple it to the ceiling as there is no space left on the walls.

25/02/07

Celtic Spirit's crew woke up in the most beautiful setting and went ashore for a walk around the sleepy town of Puerto Williams, which consists mostly of housing for the military personnel from the base and a few shops. It was Sunday so we took a taxi over to the only place that was open and serving food – the hotel where we had a delicious meal of scallops, lamb and dessert. The weather forecast was most unsuitable for a visit to Cape Horn so we decided to sail directly to our next destination, South Georgia, some 1,200 miles away. The skipper went and cleared out with the authorities. As soon as everyone was back on board and the dinghy was up, we weighed anchor and were off down the Beagle Canal for the last time. It took four hours to get to the mouth and then we were out into the ocean. The forecast was for strong winds from behind us. It was a bumpy night onboard as the boat rolled from side to side, making sleep difficult.

26/02/07

This morning brought sun and winds below 20 knots. In preparation for the strong winds forecast we rigged the storm sail and set it to

Below and right: *Vera signs our boat flag. / Boats tied up alongside the wreck and yacht club in Puerto Williams.*

Left: *(top and bottom) Michiel's drawing of the sunken ship. / The deck of the Yacht Club. /* ***Above and right:*** *Michael staples our boat flag to the ceiling. / The crew and our flag – (clockwise from top left): Vera, Michiel, Michael, Fabrizio, Ansis, Igor, Janet, JohnJohn, Denis and Blayney.*

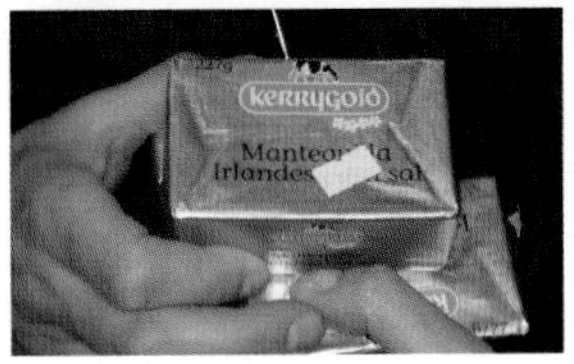

Clockwise from top left: *Replica of the* Yelco*, the vessel that rescued Shackleton's men from Elephant Island.* / *The* prefectura *offices.* *Navy ships in port.* / *The guard and his hut.* / *Michiel's drawing – the view of Puerto Williams from the top of the hill.* / *The streets of Puerto Williams.* / *(centre) Blayney finds Irish butter!* / *Fishing boats on the shore of the Beagle.*

After four or five days we left Ushuaia straight into a morning gale, 50 knots wind, 7 m high waves – a typical day in the Southern Ocean. That white stuff just came from the sky, from the clouds, from heaven, I don't know man. I felt it on my face and looked at my partners who just smiled at me and pronounced words I'd never heard before. 'It's snowing man.' It was the first snow I had ever seen and I will never forget that feeling.

Igor's diary entry

Clockwise from top left: *Sleet and snow in the Southern Ocean. / Michiel on the foredeck wearing his blue fishermans gloves to keep out the cold. / A big wave heads our way. / The waves down here reach new heights.*
Opposite page: *(top) A squall on the horizon. / (bottom from left) A view through the windows in the galley – crew reefing the mainsail. / The mast and mainsail as seen through the window from down below.*

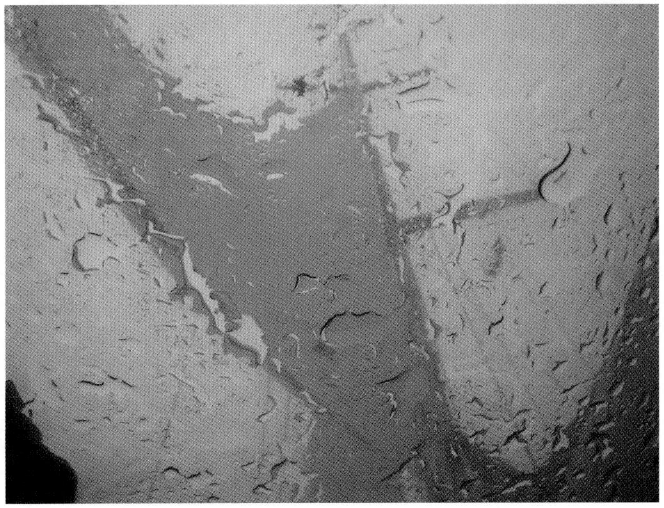

work. A dark cloud loomed on the horizon and crept slowly closer. As it hit the wind gently and steadily rose to 38 knots. It brought rain and cold but it was over within a few hours. We poled out our genny, pondering whether the system had past before us or if more strong winds were still to come. As the sun went down subtle tones of blues, pinks, mauves, purples, yellows and reds spread across the sky and darkened as sunset drew near. The sea rolled up and down in a swell that let us know who was boss as albatrosses circled up and down next to the boat. Our winds finally arrived during the night and were gusting up to 48 knots. It was another bumpy night. Our hot-blooded Brazilian crew were feeling cold and a little seasick, however, they did not realise that it would get colder when we reached the Antarctic Convergence Zone!

27/02/07

This morning's sunrise was beautiful and the wind was down to 20 knots. We put away the storm sail and poled out the genny. Later as the wind direction changed we took down the pole, tacked the genoa and raised the main. A couple of hourglass dolphins swam beside us for a while, playing on the bow wave. The morning remained sunny but it clouded over in the afternoon. The evening sky was spread with squalls that we mostly managed to avoid. Today we did 175 miles, doing on average 7.25 knots in 24 hours. During the night the winds moved around to the northwest forcing us to change our sail configuration again.

28/02/07

Today was the day of the albatross. The sea and sky were alive with them gliding up and down around the boat. Among them were black-browed albatrosses, a couple of juvenile wandering albatrosses as well as an old adult and a Southern giant petrel. At one point we passed a whole group of albatrosses sitting on the water. Watching them as they skim the surface of the water at speed is quite exhilarating. The wind was roughly around the 20-knot mark for most of the day but increased to 37 knots later. The winds stayed strong for a few hours. We have been storming along and our average today is 193 miles in 24 hours.

01/03/07

In the early hours of this morning the winds eventually died down to 25 then 20 knots and we brought out the full headsail. Our average over the last 24 hours is 150 miles. There are still loads of albatrosses with us and a lovely ocean swell. It's been a beautiful clear day. Winds remain at 20 to 25 knots. The moon appeared from over the top of the cloud casting a path of light across the playful Southern Ocean waves to the boat. The hatch door slid open and the sounds of Sweden on guitar, Netherlands on mandolin and Brazil on saxophone spilled over the top. The crew were being treated to their renditions of 'Hit The Road Jack', 'No Woman, No Cry' and 'The House of the Rising Sun' to name but a few.

The instruments were all aboard but nobody was playing them. Riding the waves eastwards with the rest of us were Michiel's mandolin, Fabrizio's sax, a set of bongos awaiting a royal manhandling from the funk-steeped paws of Igor and my own yet to be befriended fishing line strung cheap fake Spanish guitar. Though we'd been together as a group for a week or so in Ushuaia, preparing for the next leg across nowhere had kept the jamming spirit at bay. But out there somewhere in the pitch black gale of the Southern Ocean, as everyone started settling into the rhythm of wind, waves and watches, the itch-like longing for instruments broke through. Within seconds of somebody mouthing the suggestion of 'Let's play' we were all tools in hand around the saloon table. But what

Clockwise from top left: *An albatross flies across the evening sky. / Our flags are almost in shreds as we near the end of our journey. / The Antarctic moon. / JohnJohn watches as the albatross follows us.*

should we play? What would instantly unite four musicians of different nationalities, ages and backgrounds, playing together for the first time on this dark and wind-beaten piece of ocean halfway between Cape Horn and South Georgia? The answer is of course: a classic. Someone started strumming, the rest caught on and the tones of 'The House of the Rising Sun' started drifting through the companionway. And though they didn't make it far before being swallowed whole by the hungry winds of the furious fifties they had served their purpose. A band was formed. Another part of the life enhancing experience puzzle that is Celtic Spirit had been fitted with the rest.

John John's diary entry

Left and above:
Fabrizio plays his sax while Michiel plays his mandolin in the saloon. / The mandolin waits to be played.

02/03/07

Today brought winds between 30 to 40 knots from the northwest. As the wind moves around more to the west it is decided to pole out the headsails and drop the main. Four of the crew go forward to change the big pole from port to starboard, changing the uphaul over from one side to the other, untie the small pole, fix it to the mast, and attach the uphaul and downhaul. While the skipper brings the boat into the wind one crew releases the halyard and it takes two crew to pull down the main. You need to be clipped on at all times up here as waves were occasionally reaching 6 m in height and wave after wave washes over the deck. They are powerful enough to knock any person overboard. With just the genny poled out, the boat was sailing well so we decided to leave the staysail until further notice. It is a beautiful day and exhilarating: the sun shining, wind blowing, waves rolling and birds flying. The wind remains constant through out the day and the sea is big and beautiful. We are now well into the convergence zone again. The Antarctic Convergence Zone reaches up over and around South Georgia. It is much colder on the night watches and the water temperature is down to 2.6 °C. We have averaged 175 miles in the last 24 hours. The wind dies down after nightfall.

03/03/07

Throughout the night the wind increased from time to time blowing through the 40s and up to 50 knots. Early this morning it snowed briefly and the wind continued to blow over 35 knots. It began snowing again much to the delight of our Brazilian crew who had never seen snow before. It is very cold now and the sea still heaves up and down. Small mountains of water pass us by. Troughs and valleys are streaked with white foam. One wave hit us side on, throwing water into the cockpit and right over the top of the boat. This evening we spot our first icebergs this far north, they are extremely big, like a landmass. During the night the wind dies down and the sea state becomes calmer. We are approaching South Georgia and should be there tomorrow afternoon.

South Georgia

South Georgia lies within the Antarctic Convergence Zone deep in the Southern Ocean and is accessible only by sea. It is inhabited only by BAS (British Antarctic Survey) researchers and the South Georgia Government. Teeming with penguins, seals and bird life this is a most incredibly beautiful, wild and special place.

Opposite page: *Our first view of South Georgia.* / **Above and top left:** *Michiel on the bow with his shirt off excited to be reaching South Georgia.* / *The coastline of South Georgia.*

04/03/07

After eight days at sea this morning brought poor visibility, icebergs and soft rain. Slowly South Georgia became visible through the mist. The sea was full of seals and penguins. As the sun came out it cast a rainbow over the peaks. The water colour turned into a beautiful light aqua and Michiel took off his shirt, stood on the bow punching the air with his fists and shouted, 'This is South Georgia!' It turned into a stunning day and everyone was in good spirits. The wind died down to around 10 knots and so we proceeded under engine. Our first attempts at contacting the base station were met with no response. As we sailed along the north coast of the island we passed the most spectacular views of bays, mountains and glaciers. We arrived into King Edward Point, which is a British-run base, and tied up at the jetty. We cleared in and were given a briefing on the island, including the areas to stay clear of and how to treat the wildlife. The boat was cleaned down and we all enjoyed a shower. A delicious meal was made for dinner which we enjoyed with some bottles of wine and music.

After one week in the very rough Southern Ocean with blizzards, freezing conditions, 50-knot gusts and constant 35 winds, we arrived at the rocky coast. Out of the murky morning appeared the high rocky coast of South Georgia. King penguins, sea lions, sooty albatrosses all around. Sun came out and sea turns turquoise. Fantastic!

Michiel's diary entry

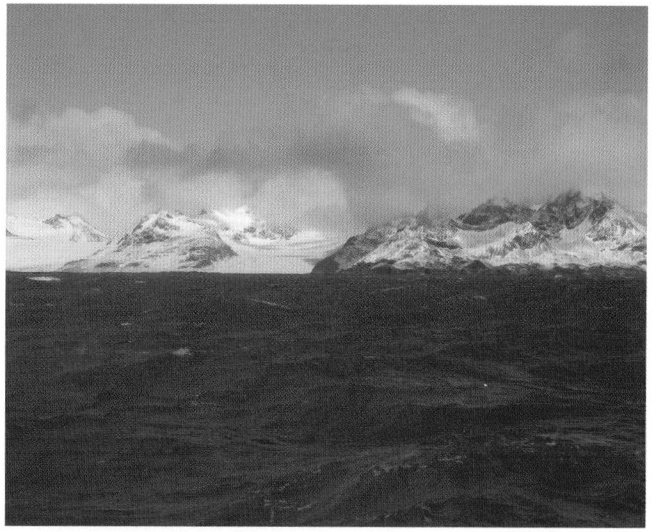

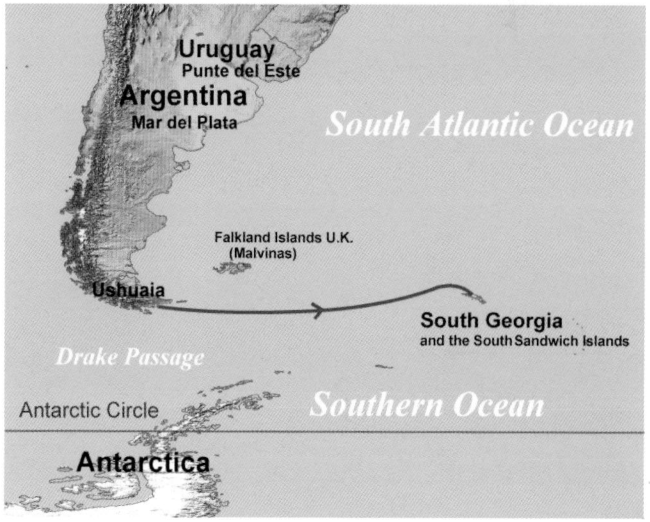

05/03/07

This morning the early risers onboard went for a walk around the base, visiting king penguins, fur seals and elephant seal pups (which are huge). It was a beautiful day, sunny and warm. They meandered off road and up the hill, along the river all the way to the top and along the ridge and down to Grytviken, the abandoned whaling station. The views were breathtaking. After a look around Grytviken the crew walked back along the road beneath the ridge that connects to King Edward Point. It is lined with fur seal pups. On return the boat was moved across from King Edward Point to the jetty at Grytviken. Here the headsail was taken down in order to do repairs and the main halyard was also repaired. Some of the crew visited the museum and Shackleton's grave. We also invited anyone who was interested from the base to come down and join us for a drink and music. Emma, head of the South Georgian government, Steve, from the British Antarctic Survey, Ainslie who runs the post office and Neil who looks after the museum at Grytviken, arrived down to the boat. They were good company and we enjoyed a great evening of live music and chat.

Clockwise from below: *Seals on the slip at King Edward Point.* / Celtic Spirit *at the pier King Edward Point.* / *Regal king penguins sunning themselves behind Shackleton Villa.* / *Blue-eyed Antarctic shags on the water's edge with a seal swimming near by.* / *The stunning views of South Georgia.*

Clockwise from top right: *South Georgia government and British Antarctic Survey buildings at King Edward Point.* / *South Georgia government harbour patrol vessel.* / *The green shed at King Edward Point.* / Celtic Spirit *tied up alongside the pier at King Edward Point, the crew and base station staff in the foreground, Grytviken in the background.* / *Another view of King Edward Point.*

Clockwise from right: *The hill above King Edward Point. / Elephant seals among the tussock grass. / Climbing the hill above King Edward Point. / A group of elephant seals lie huddled together. / The view from King Edward Point to Grytviken and the peaks behind it.*

Clockwise from above: *Looking down onto Grytviken. / Surrounding peaks. / The church behind Grytviken. / All that remains of the whaling station at Grytviken is abandoned rusty metal.*

06/03/07

Today the crew were late to rise and a little slow due to the previous night's festivities. There was a big clean up followed by a big breakfast. Afterwards everyone visited the museum, had a good look around and spent plenty of money on souvenirs in the shop. We then went over to visit the post office and Ainslie invited us for tea. We all descended on Shackleton Villa, drank lots of tea and ate all their biscuits. Ainslie made us crumpets but they were devoured faster than she could produce them and everybody began to feel very at home on the very comfortable sofas, a luxury we had not had in ages and a surprisingly pleasant experience after living on a boat at sea for a year. After returning to the boat and consuming a late dinner we went back over to the shed at King Edward Point where we had been invited to a party for a BAS staff member who was leaving the following day. It snowed quite heavily during the night.

07/03/07

It's another beautiful morning but the weather soon turned and light snow turned into quite heavy snow. The cruise ship *Hanseatic* entered the bay and before long the skipper and first mate of *Celtic Spirit* were invited aboard by its captain Ulf Wolter. It turned out that the ship's captain was a keen sailor and soon it was his turn to be shown around *Celtic Spirit*. We joked with his passengers that the captains were going to swap positions. In the afternoon the weather cleared and most of the crew went for a walk up along the river and through the valley behind the church, stopping to have a look inside before continuing. It was an easy walk along a path that

Clockwise from top right: *Blayney, Ansis, Fabrizio and Michael visit Ernest Shackleton's grave across from King Edward Point. / The graveyard where Shackleton is buried. / Shackleton's headstone. / The inscription on the back of the headstone reads 'I hold ... that a man should strive to the uttermost for his life's set prize.' Robert Browning.*

Clockwise from bottom left: *Snow at Grytviken. / A night of music and song. / Steve, Emma and Neil from the South Georgia government have a laugh. / Emma plays Fabrizio's sax. / The gin and tonics go down well. / Good company, Ainslie and Janet.*

Left: *(top to bottom) Views of Grytviken the old abandoned whaling station. |*
Above: *Ansis stops for a drink of water from the stream at Grytviken. |*
Right and far right: *Michiel and JohnJohn use our sewing machine to repair our sail. | Michiel attempts a sermon in the church at Grytviken.*

Clockwise from top left: *Curious king penguins. | Janet sits down for a chat with some friendly King penguins. | Seal pup. | More king penguins. | Seals relax on the beach. | Abandoned whale ship at Grytviken.*

Clockwise from left: *Clear, cold water streams down from the mountains. / Mist and cloud descends the mountain slopes. / Moss on the mountainside. / More snow. / Rocky mountain slopes.*

Opposite page: *(anticlockwise from top left) Snow covers everything in a white blanket. / Rocks and more rocks. / Dew drops on moss. / A view out to sea. / The sun comes out over the mountains.*

came out on top of a ridge that looks down into the next bay. The views from here are spectacular, two lakes in the valley below, sea and peaks all around. At this point some of the crew turned back while others continued on down into the valley where they came across a hut. Here they stopped for a cup of coffee, biscuits and a rest. Only one crew member made it to the shore, which was full of rather aggressive fur seal pups. Our day was rounded off by an invitation to dinner in Shackleton Villa. It was a fantastic meal with starters, main course and dessert. We drank wine, beer and Baileys coffees. We were really very spoilt. We will find it hard to leave this special place with its very hospitable inhabitants.

08/03/07

It snows every day now as we head into the autumn of the southern hemisphere. This morning we were all up early and everyone worked hard to prepare the boat for the onward journey. The morning was

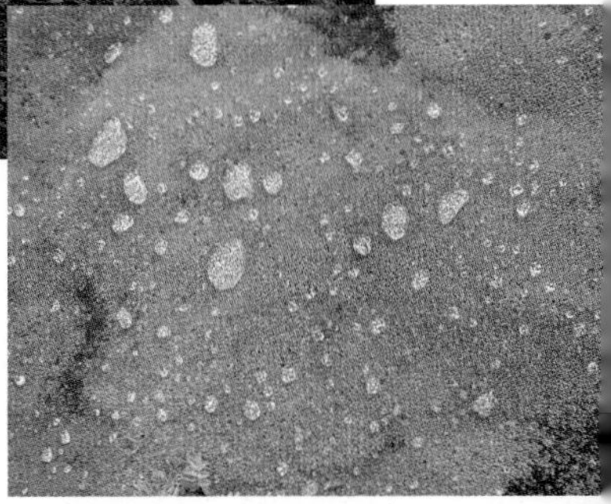

Clockwise from right: *Michael surveys the landscape of South Georgia, Michiel and Ansis behind him. / The rocky landscape of the peaks behind King Edward Point and Grytviken. / JohnJohn on top of the world at the bottom of the world.*

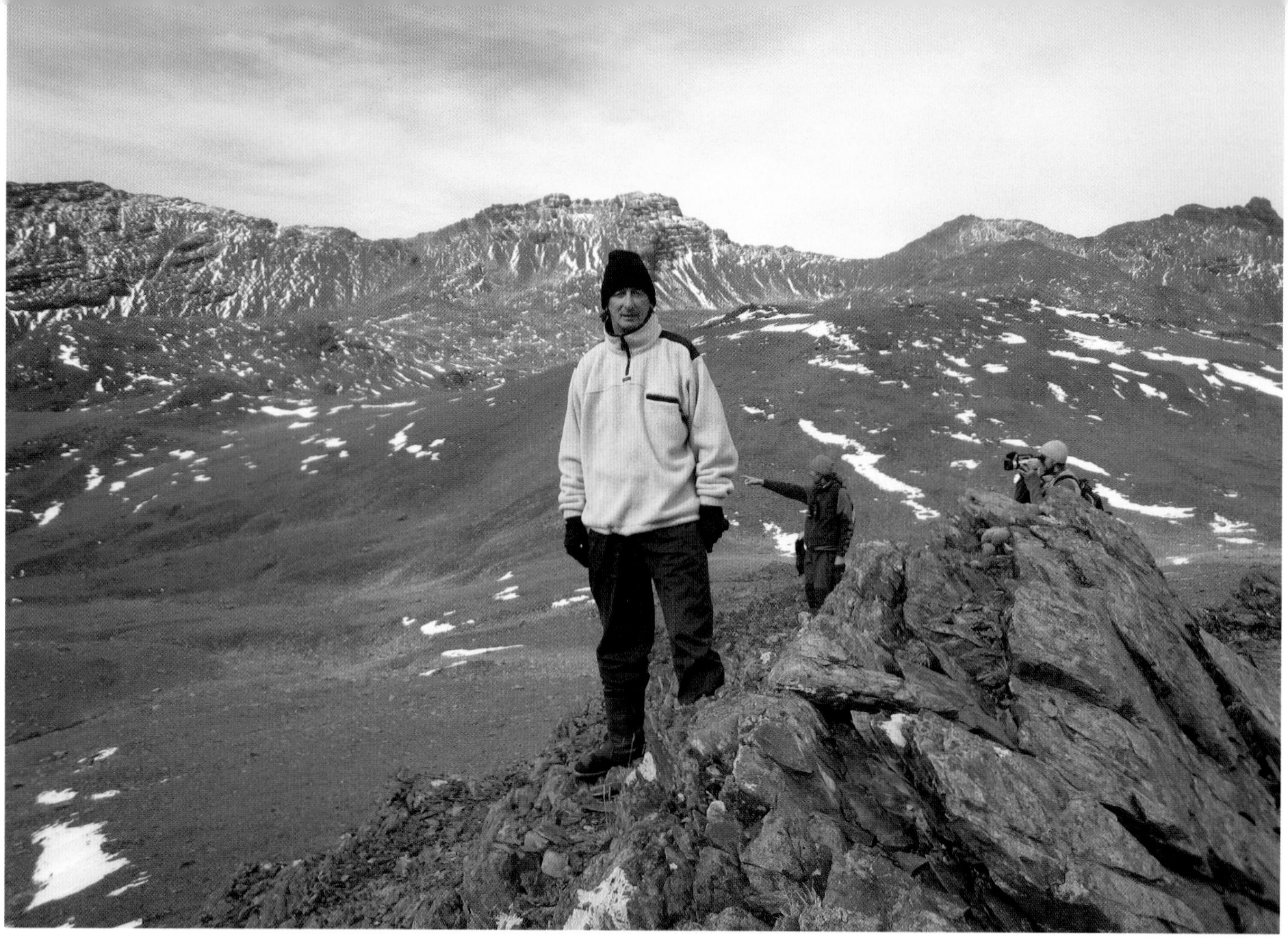

Clockwise from bottom left: *South Georgian landscape after it has snowed.* / *Michiel and Igor in the snowy peaks.* / *Fabrizio takes shelter under his space blanket next to Michiel while it snows.*

spent doing the last bits of shopping, sending postcards and saying goodbyes to the friends made in the short time of our stay. Two of the crew who had sailed with us to Antarctica, Denis and Vera, were due to arrive aboard the cruise ship *Polar Star* in the afternoon so we waited for them in order to say a brief hello. The cruise liner was delayed and so it was after 1530 before we saw the boat making its way into the bay. We ended up waving wildly to them and them to us from the deck. Our skipper had been lucky enough to speak to Denis earlier by VHF radio. After that it was back out to sea. We continued to wave sad goodbyes to South Georgia until land could no longer be seen.

Clockwise from above: Celtic Spirit *crew relax in Shackleton Villa with Ainslie, Steve and Emma. / The museum at Grytviken. / Neil and Igor with our engraved sign. / Ansis prepares another crumpet made by Ainslie.*

Left: *(from top) Fond farewells – Ansis and Ainslie. / Igor, Steve and Emma. / Mick and Ainslie. / Steve and Emma.* / **Above:** *(top and bottom) King Edward Point from the bay where we wait for the* Polar Star *to arrive. / The* Polar Star, *the cruise liner that Denis and Vera are on where they are waving to us from the top deck.*

South Georgia was to be our last stop in Antarctica thus closing the book on this epic voyage for Celtic Spirit *and her crew. It was a voyage that took nearly two years in the planning and preparation and was to take us from the Arctic to Antarctica, a distance of more than 16,000 miles covered for the most part in the last twelve months.*

From the cold seas of the northern hemisphere through the Tropics of Cancer and Capricorn and into the cold seas of the southern hemisphere we met dozens of fascinating sailors and other people from all parts of the world, many of whom are now friends we will continue to be in contact with into the future. We have travelled to some of the most beautiful and spectacular parts the world has to offer and also visited exotic islands and charismatic cities en route.

The crew experienced some of the most hostile and threatening seas of the world while enjoying the magic of trade wind sailing through tropical waters.

For all of us on board Celtic Spirit *this has been a voyage of a lifetime. For many it has been a life-changing experience and for all of us to have shared this incredible voyage has forever bound us together as we earned our place in King Neptune's Court.*

Michael Holland, Skipper

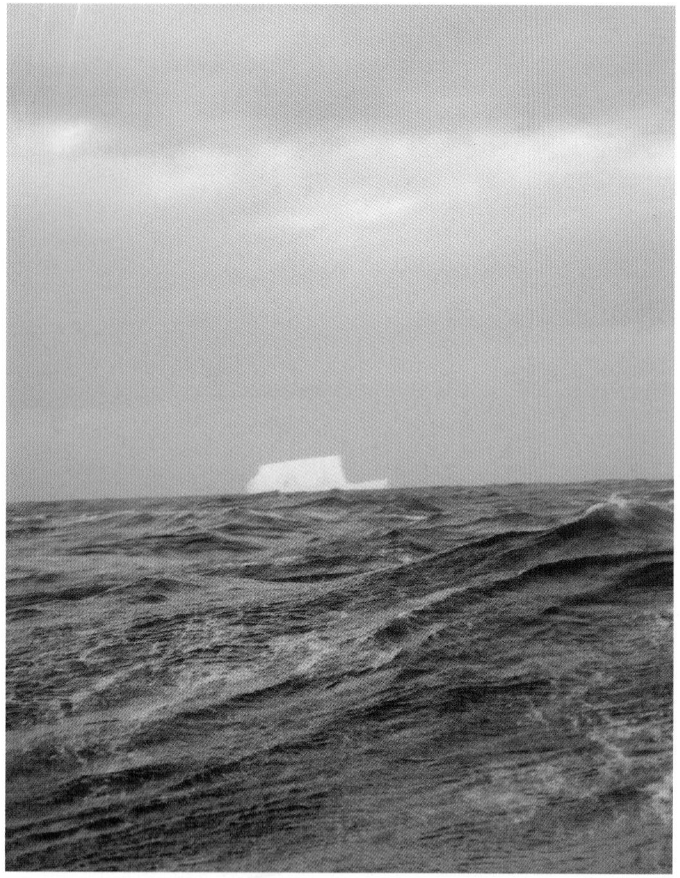

I am more terrified by ice the more I come across it. This passage out of South Georgia has been the worst to date. Moving ice fields at night awakens one's senses to the possibility of sudden and unimaginable consequences of being holed by ice and an almost certain watery grave. We are all intimidated and humbled by this nature. Some of the ice is translucent and almost invisible.

Skipper's diary entry